It's hard to imagine a time when the Eastside didn't abound with shopping malls, high-tech businesses and sprawling suburban neighborhoods.

Yet, only a century ago it was coal mining, not computers, that drew workers east across Lake Washington. Decades before that, when huge, old-growth forests covered the land from lake to mountains, it was loggers who built the first towns and cleared the land for the bountiful farming era that was to follow.

The pages of Eastside history are rich with stories of pioneers and entrepreneurs whose dreams shaped the communities of yesteryear: Peter Kirk and his vision of a steel-mill empire in what is now downtown Kirkland; George Washington Tibbets and the hop farms that spawned an industry in the Snoqualmie Valley.

In this edition, we've added chapters on the immigrant waves that shaped the region's populace, the building of the Eastside's major highway and the ongoing lure of the "Gold Coast" communities, among others.

These are the stories of the Eastside's Hidden Past. Whaling ships in Meydenbauer Bay? Yes, for decades. Indian long houses on Mercer Slough? Sure. Rowdy frontier towns? Bootleg liquor in Bellevue and moonshine stills in Kirkland?

Yes, the Eastside does indeed have a history. Come walk through a few of its pages and catch a glimpse of how it all began.

A HIDDEN PAST

AN EXPLORATION OF EASTSIDE HISTORY

The complete collection of a series that was published in The Seattle Times from December 1997 to January 2000, plus eight new chapters in this revised and expanded 2002 edition.

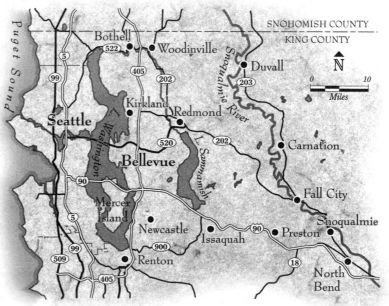

THE SEATTLE TIMES

On the cover and above:
Postmistress Isabel Bechtel and daughters Maude and Jessie are photographed about 1900 in front of their log cabin, which was Bellevue's second post office. This photo is from The Seattle Times photo archives.

TABLE OF CONTENTS

ACKNOWLEDGMENTS

Editor: Arlene Bryant ◆ **Copy editors:** Don Kirkpatrick, Marilyn Bailey, Sandy Dunham
Designers: Denise Clifton, Aldo Chan ◆ **Production:** Seattle Times Imaging Department

COPYRIGHT 2002

The Seattle Times

seattletimes.com

ISBN: 0-949912-07-9

CHAPTER 1

PEOPLE OF THE MOON

The Snoqualmies were once one of the largest and most feared tribes in the area

MARYMOOR MUSEUM OF EASTSIDE HISTORY

Deep in the Valley of the Moon, there is music: the sound of water from Snoqualmie Falls crashing to the hard earth and the wind whistling through stands of cedar and fir. There is peace out here where the first people of the Eastside chased the seasons and looked to the sky, hoping to find their creator lounging in the crook of a crescent moon.

They are known as the Snoqualmie Indians, once one of the biggest and most feared tribes in the Puget Sound area. The Snoqualmies, who recently received federal recognition, make up one of two main tribes that call the Eastside home.

A certain sense of peace remains in the Snoqualmie Valley, more than 140 years after a treaty signed between Native Americans and white settlers caused whole villages to be erased from the map — villages that once hunkered along lakes and rivers throughout the Eastside.

The Eastside was not stereotypical Indian country, with smoke swirling out of tepees or Native Americans carving totem poles. Instead, the landscape was dotted with cedar-shake cabins and long houses that held 30 to 40 people.

Many roads that now cut through the Eastside originally were Indian trails. The forests now being stripped away to make room for homes were a supermarket of sorts for Native Americans, providing them with deer and mountain goats, salmonberries and tiger-lily bulbs.

Areas closest to Lake Washington, where Bellevue, Kirkland and Redmond are now, were not considered Indian country, although there were traces of Native-American life through the 1850s.

The long houses were torn down to make room for encroaching white homesteaders.

A couple of long houses once stood near Yarrow Bay, and two others were at the tip of Mercer Slough, close to where Interstate 90 and 118th Avenue Southeast are now. Warriors from Central Washington slept and stored supplies there during the Indian War of 1856, according to historical accounts.

Native Americans pick hops in the Snoqualmie Valley around 1890. Many worked on the farms of white settlers.

BY PUTSATA REANG

Land swapped in treaty

As part of the Point Elliott Bay Treaty of 1855, tribes in the Puget Sound region swapped hundreds of acres of their land, much of which was on the Eastside, with white settlers in exchange for reservation land elsewhere and certain privileges, including fishing rights.

Angry at the terms, some Native American groups began warring with white settlers shortly after the signing of the treaty. But the settlers, with the help of the Snoqualmie Indians, squashed splinter groups that were battling them. Eventually, most Indians moved to crowded Western Washington reservations set up by the federal government.

Many who left their homes came back to the Eastside in the late 1800s to make money working the hop fields of white farmers.

Eastside towns including Issaquah, Fall City, Snoqualmie and Carnation served as cultural junctions for Native Americans back when hop farms covered vast stretches of land on the Issaquah Valley floor and in the Snoqualmie Valley.

More than 1,000 Native Americans were recruited to pick hops at a 1,500-acre valley farm known as the Hop Ranch, a spread known today as the Meadowbrook Farm.

Records from the late 1880s indicate Native Americans came from as far away as Alaska and Yakima, by canoe and pony, to work the fields.

A hop louse that swept through the region in the early 1900s wiped out the entire Eastside hop industry, and the Indians turned to logging.

The dark, rich soil in the Snoqualmie Valley was ideal for other crops, including potatoes.

Leona Eddy, a 79-year-old Snoqualmie elder, remembers the backbreaking labor of digging small fingers into the dirt and pulling up the vegetable by the root.

"There was such huge big potatoes raised up and down the valley there," Eddy recalls.

She worked beside her grandfather, Jerry Kanim, who was the last lineal chief of the Snoqualmie Tribe.

The inception of the Native American Shaker religion occurred during the hop craze, founded by a couple from the Olympia area who were part of the annual migration east to work the fields.

Mary Slocum, wife of John Slocum, a Squaxin Indian who claimed he died but was refused entry into heaven and instead was sent back to exhort others to abandon their sins, introduced the practice of shaking during worship, which was said to rid people of ailments and sin.

The religion worked its way into the lives of many Snoqualmie Indians, including Eddy. "Grandma had the Shaker church in our home," Eddy said.

Native Americans jammed into the tiny home in

SNOQUALMIE TRIBAL ARCHIVES

Mary Louie, great-great-grandmother of tribal elder Leona Eddy, was a Snoqualmie medicine woman. She died at age 120 in 1918, the year after this photo was taken.

MARYMOOR MUSEUM OF EASTSIDE HISTORY

Snoqualmie Falls in 1899

THE STORY OF THE MOON

"It happened a long time before anyone wrote anything down. The Moon Child, Snoqualm, said goodbye to his wife in the western ocean and walked up the river toward the home of his mother, wife of the Red Star.

"As Moon walked up the river he confronted fierce monsters. He transformed them into plants and animals to create a home where the people could live. When he came to the place where Raven had built a fish weir across the river, Moon turned that fish weir into stone.

"At this place with the river pouring over the lip of the stone, Moon created the first man and woman, then climbed into the sky to stay. Forever."

— A version of the creation myth of the Snoqualmie Tribe, as told in the documentary video "For All People, For All Time."

Carnation, where Eddy was raised. They broke into a feverish sweat as they violently shook their bodies to stamp out all things evil.

Many Native Americans practiced the religion privately in each other's homes until 1892, when the Slocums and their followers incorporated their movement as the Indian Shaker Church, giving it legal status.

The religion took off and Shaker churches still can be found on Native American reservations throughout the state.

Other tribes

The Duwamish Indians are the other tribe whose homeland is found on the Eastside. Their villages once lined the water's edge along the southern shores of Lake Washington, lands that now are the industrial shoulders that support the city of Renton.

Members of the Duwamish Tribe still live in the Renton area. They are currently appealing a decision by the U.S. Bureau of Indian Affairs that denied them federal recognition.

Although only two tribes lived on the Eastside, many Native American communities sprung up around lakes and rivers, including Lakes Sammamish and Washington, and the Snoqualmie and Cedar rivers.

They were known as hah-chu ah bsh, or "lake people," and they represented tribes east of the Cascades and around the Puget Sound area that set up temporary villages along these waterways, following their food supply. "The water was the centerpoint for life," said Greg Watson, director of the Snoqualmie Valley Historical Society.

Native Americans used the waterways to travel to trade with other Indians, to fish and to bathe.

European settlers homesteaded in clearings where Native Americans had laid down leather blankets to sleep under the open sky.

Road routes, such as the Interstate 90 corridor,

SNOQUALMIE TRIBAL ARCHIVES

Charlie Walker was a Snoqualmie tribal secretary in the early 1900s. He is standing in a traditional dug-out canoe, most likely on the Tolt River.

came courtesy of Native American guides who showed early settlers how to get to such places as Snoqualmie Falls and how to get past the huge mountain walls of the Cascades.

"We're following, quite literally, in Native American footsteps," Watson said.

CHAPTER 2

BLACK DIAMONDS

By the 1870s Newcastle was the center of a bustling mining economy

It was an economic boom that lasted for more than 50 years — one that helped put Seattle and the Eastside on the map.

And it was a force that almost overnight turned this part of the Pacific Northwest into an ethnic melting pot.

Described in newspapers of the day, it was called "coal rush" and "coal fever."

Coal. Black diamonds. Black gold.

RENTON HISTORICAL MUSEUM

It didn't replace the growing logging industry, but the discovery of coal in Issaquah and Newcastle in the early 1860s strengthened the region's economic backbone and turned Seattle into a thriving port of call.

Miners by the hundreds, mostly immigrants from Europe, flocked to the infant towns of Newcastle, Coal Creek and Renton. In a way, they were pioneers, first- and second-generation folks from Wales, Finland, Italy, England, Scotland, Ireland, Belgium, Croatia and Slovakia.

They lived in small settlements — Coal Creek, Red Town, Finn Town and Rainbow Town — separated by culture and national origin. They labored in mines with names such as Primrose, Bagley, May Creek, Muldoon and Jones.

Scratching a meager living from beneath the forested hills that sprawled across the Eastside, the men and boys often worked on their hands and knees, crawling along tunnels and thin, sloping coal veins, lighted only by the meager flicker from carbide lamps attached to the front of their helmets.

Coal was discovered on Squak Mountain in Issaquah

A Newcastle coal-mine rescue team in 1924 included, from left, B.F. Snook (the captain), George Hasku, Walter Clark, Joe Ansberger and George Munson.

This was Newcastle in 1883. The town had a population of about 750, which included 310 who were on the mining-company payroll.

THEODORE PEISER / MUSEUM OF HISTORY & INDUSTRY

BY LOUIS T. CORSALETTI

in 1859, but it wasn't until 1862 that L.B. Andrews and W.W. Perkins brought several loads to Seattle. The next year coal was found in Coal Creek on the west side of Cougar Mountain.

Newcastle became the center of the newly established industry by the late 1860s and early 1870s, with the towns of Coal Creek and Coalfield nearby.

Mine tunnels soon were dug throughout what is now known as the Issaquah Alps between Issaquah and Lake Washington.

Local newspapers referred to King County as the Pennsylvania of the West.

It was a time when Seattle was essentially a port of call for shipping timber from the vast forests that blanketed the Eastside foothills. Underneath much of that land was coal, millions of tons of black diamonds.

At first, the coal was moved via tramways, wagons, canoes and barges to docks at King and Pike streets in Seattle, where it was loaded onto ships bound for San Francisco and, later, to Hawaii and Australia.

In 1878 the Seattle and Walla Walla Railroad was punched through to the mines, but it wasn't until a few years later when the Northern Pacific Railroad connected to the area that the national-market boom began.

By the 1880s coal was king and Newcastle was the second-largest city in King County, rivaled only by Seattle. The thriving community was producing about 200,000 tons of coal annually.

Newcastle's fame had spread to the extent that when President Rutherford B. Hayes came to Washington Territory in 1880, accompanied by Gen. William Tecumseh Sherman of Civil War fame, he insisted on visiting Newcastle.

Death lurked in the dark, damp and cold working spaces of the deep mines. Methane gas and dust

The Coal Creek Mine, shown here around 1900, was hit by a fire in December 1894. About 160 miners escaped without injury.

explosions, cave-ins and accidents were not common but occurred often enough to take a toll. Four men were killed and four others seriously injured in an explosion in October 1894.

Quentin Hyatt was the last miner killed in Newcastle, while working for the B & R Co. in 1951. That company closed the last diggings at Newcastle in 1963, according to "The Coals of Newcastle," a book by Richard McDonald and Lucile McDonald.

By the mid-1960s, a string of mining companies — Pacific Coast Coal, Lake Washington Coal, Seattle Coal and Strain Coal — had removed more than 10 million tons of coal from the Newcastle fields. But long before that, nature began regenerating the raped land.

Little is left to remind today's generation of what once was the small area's 15 minutes of fame. A 117-year-old wood-frame structure known as the Baima house still stands in today's Newcastle, along with a small segment of the foundation of a hotel, a sealed-off entrance to a tunnel, piles of slag and rock now covered with alder and ferns, a tipple (an apparatus for emptying coal) and concrete foundations for a steam-powered hoisting engine at the Ford Slope.

Routes of Newcastle coal to Seattle

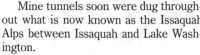

·······	1865 Wagon and canoe
—·—·—	1866-1870 Tram and barges
— — —	1870-1878 Steamboat and tram
┼┼┼┼┼	1878-1930 Narrow-gauge and later standard- gauge railroad

Seattle Bellevue

Elliott Bay

Lake Washington

Mercer Island

Lake Sammamish

Newcastle

Issaquah

Coal Creek

Duwamish Waterway

Renton

N

0 Miles 5

Cedar River

THE SEATTLE TIMES

RENTON HISTORICAL MUSEUM

Information from "The Coals of Newcastle" by Richard McDonald and Lucile McDonald is included in this report and map.

CHAPTER 3

LOST TOWNS

Coal and lumber towns that once shored up the local economy have vanished

Say "Eastside history" and some people snicker. The subdivisions, corporate campuses and shopping centers look too new, too recent, for historical roots.

But before Bellevue Square and Redmond Town Center, there were company stores and Native American trading grounds on the Eastside. Long before Microsoft, lumber companies shored up the local economy.

MARYMOOR MUSEUM OF EASTSIDE HISTORY

Eastside development didn't start when Lake Washington was spanned by a bridge but when entrepreneurs looked at the giant trees that covered the land between Lake Washington and the Cascade Mountains, the water running in the valleys and the coal under the hills — and saw gold.

Workers saw jobs.

Together they created such places as Redtown, Donnelly, Monohon, Snoqualmie Falls, Taylor and Moncton.

When the lumber was gone and the mines closed, some towns survived. Others changed names or were absorbed by bigger towns. Some simply disappeared.

Donnelly, for instance, was a sawmill settlement at the southwestern end of Lake Sammamish in the 1870s. Today only piling remains where barges once picked up lumber and carried it up the lake, through the Sammamish River and into Lake Washington to Seattle.

Taylor, an industrial town in the Cedar River watershed, once housed 900 workers and their families. It was condemned and shut down in 1945.

Kerriston, southeast of Preston, boasted a population of 400 during the Eastside's logging heyday in the early 1900s. A few deserted houses, a church and an old schoolhouse marked the site in the early 1950s, when David and Nancy Horrocks of Issaquah stumbled upon it.

"We looked in the window of the schoolhouse, and everything was there waiting, like it had been left for students," Nancy Horrocks said. "There were even McGuffey Readers on the desks."

Remnants of the town of Moncton lie beneath Rattlesnake Lake just south of Interstate 90 near North Bend.

Local historians have preserved some records of the Eastside's lost towns, enough to show how development of the area's communities happened in stages:

First came a handful of homesteaders, followed by a few sawmill and logging villages. The logging operations cleared the land, opening it to mining of coal, clay and gravel. The farms came later, eventually disappearing as subdivisions and business parks sprouted in their place.

How many sawmills were there? Dozens and dozens.

Tiger Mountain near Issaquah was ringed by about 100 sawmills during the logging years. About eight mills operated between 1890 and 1930 in the Redmond area. An early Bellevue mill stood about where City Hall is today. When an area was logged out, companies packed up their sawmill machinery and moved to a new site.

Much of the Eastside wood was shipped east via rail, although some stayed closer to home and trussed

This view taken around 1900 looking northwest toward Lake Sammamish shows the company town of Monohon, which thrived from the late 1800s to the mid 1920s.

BY SHERRY GRINDELAND

Taylor's factory sits in the foreground of this 1908 photograph.

up decades of building in the Northwest.

What was life like in the lost towns?

In 1915, when roads were mere muddy paths, you could catch a train in Moncton and spend the afternoon shopping in Seattle.

If you lived in 1906 in High Point, between what is now Preston and Issaquah, you could mail a letter at the local post office and stop to visit a traveling salesman at the hotel. Inside the High Point mill, when men could make themselves heard above the machinery, they spoke Swedish. Owner John Lovgren hired only Swedish immigrants.

"It made a cohesive community," says history buff Eric Erickson of Issaquah. "They didn't have the turnover in workers many other mills had."

The policy earned the town its nickname: Little Sweden.

If you were a coal miner in Newcastle during the 1890s, your children learned to read in the town school that served this thriving community of about 1,000 people. You could go to the community's church on Sunday.

At Snoqualmie Falls from the 1920s to the 1950s, scrap wood filled the woodshed behind your six-room company house — four on the main floor and two in the attic — plus an outhouse.

Bachelors usually lived in communal bunkhouses or dormitories. Japanese workers often had separate dormitories.

Going to Seattle was a popular Saturday night activity for the mill workers in the early part of this century, Erickson says. Railroads, which crisscrossed much of the Eastside, would run Saturday night trains to bring workers into Seattle. On Sunday afternoons the foreman would go into Seattle and round up his crew, bringing them back on the final night train so they'd be ready to work Mondays.

Life in the company towns was a mixed bag, recalled Walt Seil of Issaquah, whose father worked at the Snoqualmie Falls sawmill.

"We literally owed our soul to the company store," he said. "You bought everything there."

But the company took care of workers and their families, he said, providing for medical care at the company hospital, education in the company school and a social life at the community center.

Traces of the Eastside's lost towns still can be found. A Monohon sign designates the former stop on the railroad tracks along East Lake Sammamish Parkway.

A few High Point houses remain on a dead-end road north of I-90. In 1910, Erickson's father was born in one of those houses. The former schoolhouse has become a church, and all of the visible houses on the road have been remodeled. The town's footprint, including the mill pond, was buried under I-90 at Exit 20.

Many Eastside maps contain former town names as area designations. Physical evidence may have disappeared, but the past lives on in neighborhood names.

WHERE ARE THEY NOW? OLD TOWNS, NEW NAMES

Some early Eastside communities began under different names. Redmond, for example, was once known as Salmonberg. Mercer Island was originally East Seattle. Here are others that have changed over the years:

Beaumont: An early name for the Bellevue area that includes Beaux Arts and Enatai.

Cherry Valley: Now goes by Duvall, named for loggers James and Francis Duvall, who settled there in 1871.

Gilman: The inland portion of Issaquah until 1895.

Houghton: Once a separate incorporated community, now part of Kirkland. In 1880 it was one of three Eastside towns.

Hubbard: An early name for Juanita.

Moorland: On early maps this designated the areas now known as Meydenbauer Bay, Medina and Clyde Hill.

Salmonberg: Redmond had this moniker until 1881, when it officially became Melrose. It was renamed Redmond in 1883.

Squak: The lakefront portion of Issaquah.

Squak Lake: Lake Sammamish.

St. Louis: An early name for Preston.

Tolt: Changed to Carnation in recognition of the milk company that opened a major farm nearby.

Eastside communities that are mostly gone

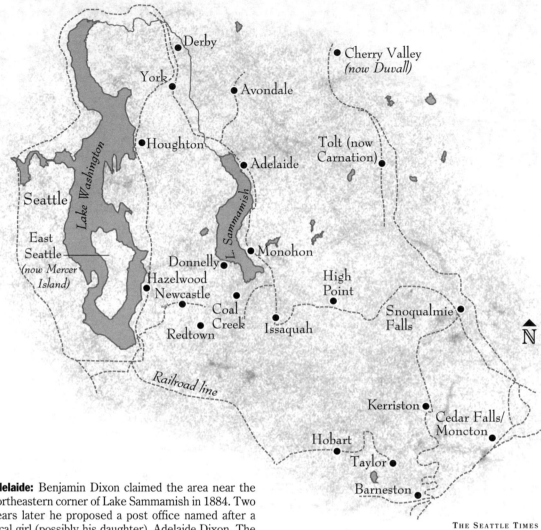

THE SEATTLE TIMES

Adelaide: Benjamin Dixon claimed the area near the northeastern corner of Lake Sammamish in 1884. Two years later he proposed a post office named after a local girl (possibly his daughter), Adelaide Dixon. The Campbell Mill opened here in 1905 and was destroyed by fire in the early 1920s.

Avondale: Four homesteaders named this small settlement near the junction of Bear and Cottage Lake creeks around 1890. An early business was a legal whiskey distillery.

Barneston: This sawmill town in the Cedar River watershed got a post office in 1901, and the entire town was torn down in 1924. It was named for John G. Barnes, a Seattle businessman.

Cedar Falls: After Seattle wells ran dry in the Great Seattle Fire of 1889, city fathers looked to the Cedar River for a reliable and clean water supply, buying up to 45,000 surrounding acres by 1911. The town of Cedar Falls was built by Seattle City Light to house construction workers for its first power plant. Today three houses, street lights and a dilapidated tennis court remain.

Coal Creek: This community 1½ miles east of Newcastle flourished as a coal-mining village from the 1880s until the 1920s. Between the two communities there were 3,000 residents, dance halls, stores, schools and barbershops.

Derby: In 1905, homesteaders in the northern end of the Sammamish Valley caught trains for Bothell or Seattle in Derby. The settlement had a store, dance hall and schoolhouse. A big brick schoolhouse replaced the original wooden structure in 1912, and today drivers along Woodinville-Redmond Road Northeast recognize it as the Hollywood Schoolhouse. Derby was renamed Hollywood by Frederick Stimson, who built the schoolhouse and named it after the numerous holly trees he had planted on the logged-over hill. Stimson's dairy farm is now the site of the Chateau Ste. Michelle winery.

Donnelly: In the 1870s, a small community developed on the southwest end of Lake Sammamish, near the mouth of Lewis Creek. Sometimes noted on maps as Donelly's, the settlement included the sawmill and a dock. When the surrounding area was logged out in 1889, the sawmill was dismantled and moved to the east side of Lake Sammamish.

Hazelwood: The post office, town, railway station and boat landing that were here in 1907 have been replaced by Interstate 405 and the Lake Washington shoreline neighborhood of Pleasure Point in South Bellevue.

High Point: In 1906, 40 sawmill employees and their families lived in this small valley town between Preston and Issaquah. The High Point mill and logging camps burned in 1922 but were rebuilt. The mill burned again in 1932, was rebuilt in 1935 and became the Tiger Mountain Sawmill in 1949.

Hobart: First settled in the late 1870s, this sawmill town faded after the mill burned in the mid-1930s. Once it had a hotel, a store, houses and a railroad station. Today it is a neighborhood south of Issaquah, with a store and fire station.

Kerriston: This sawmill town southeast of Preston was named after founder and mill owner Albert Kerry. He was a leading Seattle resident and built the Olympic Hotel, now the Four Seasons Olympic. During the heyday of Eastside and South King County logging, Kerriston was home to 400 people. It ceased operation in 1943.

Moncton: Near the remains of Cedar Falls, this former Native American trading ground was logged and farmed, and became a railroad community in the early part of the century when the Chicago, Milwaukee, St. Paul and Pacific Railroad was built through Snoqualmie Pass. When the Cedar River was blocked to form Cedar Lake — now Chester Morse Lake — seepage through glacial moraine slowly flooded Moncton. Today foundations of the school, gymnasium, indoor swimming pool, post office and houses lie under Rattlesnake Lake.

Monohon: In 1889 the saws and equipment from Donnelly were moved to the eastern shore of Lake Sammamish. A company town grew up around it, housing several hundred people in the first half of this century. At one time the company owned 120 acres of property along the lake and up the hill toward the Sammamish Plateau. A spectacular fire burned much of the town in 1925. Named after Martin Monohon, who homesteaded a ranch there in 1871, the town was where today's East Lake Sammamish Parkway and Northeast 33rd Street intersect.

Newcastle: There's old Newcastle and new Newcastle. Coal was king in the old Newcastle, the second-largest community in King County in the 1880s. About 1,000 people, miners and their families lived in the company town. Bellevue farmers went to Newcastle to vote on Election Day, and off-duty miners played pool and drank beer in local saloons. The original town faded away by the 1930s. The new Newcastle, in the same general area, incorporated in 1994 and covers a 4.5-square-mile area between Bellevue and Renton.

RENTON HISTORICAL MUSEUM

Redtown: A mining settlement near Newcastle in what is now the Cougar Mountain Regional Wildland Park was 750 people strong in 1912. Today an old sign, on the Cougar Mountain trails, points the direction to the site.

Snoqualmie/Snoqualmie Falls: Today's Snoqualmie was platted in 1889 as Snoqualmie Falls. It became Snoqualmie almost instantly. So the name Snoqualmie Falls was available when Weyerhaeuser developed a company town a mile north, across the Snoqualmie River. It existed from 1917 to the mid-1950s and had the first Eastside mill powered by electricity. At the peak, 250 families lived in the company town. The houses were sold and moved in 1958, and a bulldozer destroyed the community center, hospital and other surplus buildings.

Taylor: The need for water and sewage pipes along the West Coast built Taylor. Nearby deposits of clay for the pipe and coal to power the production plant made it an ideal industrial community when it was started by the Renton-Denny Coal Co. in 1893 about eight miles east of Maple Valley. During the height of production, 39 boxcars of pipe and brick were shipped each week. The company's mines, in the Cedar River watershed, about four miles from Hobart, were flooded in the 1920s. Gladding, McBean and Co. took over the production in 1927. Pollution from outhouses for the 900 workers and their families and from pipe and brick production were too close to Seattle's water supply, and the town was condemned and shut down in 1945.

York: A gleam in an investor's eye, this town never amounted to more than a mark on early maps, a train station and a few homes. The name first appeared on 1880 title maps, according to the late Lucile McDonald, a local historian. It was near Redmond, along the western edge of the Sammamish Valley by Willows Road and just south of Northeast 124th Street. By 1906 the land, like the rest of the Sammamish Valley, was used for dairy farming.

Miners wait to head underground at the head of Coal Creek's Ford Slope in 1920. Gustav Holma, in the front end of the coal car looking through the railings, lived with his family in Redtown, one of several small settlements during the coal-mining heyday.

Seattle Times librarians Cathy Donaldson and Stephen Selter contributed to this report.

CHAPTER 4

STILLWATER'S STORY

When timber was king, loggers' camps became cities on the hillsides

DARIUS KINSEY

Loggers, above, line the rail spur at Stillwater Camp. In the background are tents used by the loggers. Off to the right would be the Stillwater Store.

It's not much more than a wide spot on the highway now, but before the turn of the century and into the 1930s, Stillwater was one of those Eastside communities riding the crest of the logging industry.

Today, at least one of the first permanent buildings — the Stillwater Store — remains to remind travelers on Highway 203 of those days when timber was king.

When the first settlers arrived, the land from the banks of the Snoqualmie River inland to the upper valley river basin was covered with a dense growth of trees — maple, cedar and hazel. On the surrounding hilltops was the prize — stands of towering evergreen trees.

It was like a gold rush. By the late 1800s, numerous logging camps and sawmills sprouted throughout the valley, stretching from Cherry Valley north of Duvall, south through Carnation, Snoqualmie, Snoqualmie Falls and long-disappeared logging towns along the east shore of Lake Sammamish called Adelaide, Monohon and High Point.

TOLT HISTORICAL SOCIETY

At left, the original building housing the Stillwater Fair (now Stillwater Store) was built just after 1900 by Horace Chipman. The post office was put in the store in 1910.

Stillwater, about three miles north of Carnation, was one of those logging centers.

Loggers swarmed over the hills above Stillwater, downing the huge trees at a breakneck pace. The air was filled with the singsong drone of saws slicing through virgin timber and the echo of axes biting into tree trunks.

Tent cities soon mushroomed. An assortment of logging companies marked the work fest — Cherry Valley Logging, Security Logging, Stephens Bird,

BY LOUIS T. CORSALETTI

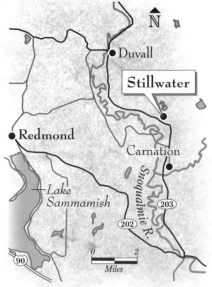

Campbell, Swan's and Jones Lumber.

Early on, logs were slid down hillsides at Stillwater, pulled by horses to the river's edge and floated, and later barged, downriver to Monroe or Everett.

The backbreaking work lessened a bit by 1911 when the Chicago, Milwaukee and St. Paul railroad ran a spur from its main line between Monroe and Carnation. The spur ran right through the logging camp unofficially known as Stillwater.

Story behind the name

But where did the name come from?

There is no written history about Stillwater, but at least one historical source tells of a group of loggers who migrated west from Stillwater, Minn., and brought the name with them. They were veterans of Minnesota's white pine and oak forests, where Stillwater was one of the biggest timber producers in the nation at the time.

Horace Chipman, who lived in the valley area, is said to have built the store building in the early 1900s. When a post office was opened in the store in 1910, the postmaster, H. Butikofer, chose the name Stillwater, though the community never was incorporated.

The arrival of the railroad in 1911 made it easier to log the hills around Stillwater. By 1930, the area was logged out and the Stillwater logging camp was shut down.

Part of the rail spur, which once ran in front of the Stillwater Store, eventually became the bed for a section of Highway 203. Remnants of a short bridge carrying the rail spur from the main line can be seen on the west side of Highway 203, just north of the store, where several wood pillars stick out in pairs from a wetland.

Stillwater grew and eventually a school was built.

At first, loggers lived in tents and makeshift shacks.

By 1915, bunkhouses were built at the camp at the bottom of Stillwater Hill. In 1920, a small hotel and machine shop were added on what is now Highway 203.

Stillwater School

Mildred Pickering lived in Novelty, above Stillwater, and drove her Ford Model T to Stillwater School to teach fifth- through eighth-graders from 1928 to 1932.

Pickering said she arrived at the school as a bride after graduating from Bellingham Normal School, now Western Washington University.

"Naturally, it was very different in schools those days. I had to get there by 8 a.m., build a fire in the stove and haul water from several blocks away," she recalled.

Pickering, who lives in Carnation, said there were 18 students in the school, which was located on a road cut into the hillside running parallel to the rail spur, just above the Stillwater Store. Many students took the Stillwater School Bus, driven at one time by Paddy Wilhite, who lived in Novelty.

By 1930, the hills were logged out and the Stillwater logging camp was closed down. But the Stillwater Store and about three or four houses, built near the end of the logging boom, survived.

Carl Buse bought the store in 1943. He died three years later, and it changed hands several times until his son Gene bought it in 1967.

Gene Buse and his wife, Marge, ran the store for some 26 years before selling it. As they watched the Lower Snoqualmie Valley grow, they changed the mom-and-pop operation to the modern convenience store it is today.

Paddy Wilhite drove students from the Novelty and Stillwater area to the Stillwater School in this bus.

CHAPTER 5

BOTHELL

Rooted in logging and farming, it became one of the Eastside's liveliest towns

DARIUS KINSEY / BOTHELL HISTORICAL MUSEUM

Logging drew men to Bothell in the 1880s. The man sitting second from left is believed to be David Bothell, who filed the first plat in the future city.

It was a valley occupied by cougars and bears, a valley where few whites had ventured. But the virgin land by the Sammamish River would belong to men like George Brackett, settlers who looked into the dense, dark forest and saw their futures.

They cut the timber and floated the logs down to Lake Washington and to sawmills in Seattle.

They took the two natural resources — the trees and the river — and turned them into a livelihood, a job, a home and soon a community of loggers living in log homes by the river.

And when fires took down their man-made structures over and over, the settlers just rebuilt.

"They were not going to be driven away that easily," said local historian Regan Sidie.

Instead, those early pioneers brought relatives and friends from Seattle, folks with Scandinavian and Midwestern roots, and solidified the community.

The Bothells

David Bothell was among the dozens of early settlers who came to Brackett's logging camp in the 1880s.

The Pennsylvania Civil War veteran and his wife, Mary Anne, in 1889 filed the first plat in what later became known as Bothell. They built a shingle mill and created jobs, many filled by East Europeans.

The couple lived at what is now the downtown corner of 101st Avenue Northeast and Northeast 183rd Street. They ran a boarding house and later a hotel.

The Bothells raised seven children and became a fixture in the community.

When asked what to call the area, the postmaster figured it should be Bothell since there were so many of them. And it was incorporated as Bothell in 1909.

George and Alice Bothell. George's parents settled in the area in the 1880s.

BY TAN VINH

This 1894 photo of downtown Bothell looks west down Main Street. Many of the trees in the background would be cut a decade later.

SEATTLE TIMES ARCHIVES

By then the community had two shingle factories, a broom-handle mill, four general stores, two hotels, three meat markets, a bakery, a barber shop and three saloons.

By 1910 Bothell counted 599 residents, contained mostly around what is still Main Street.

That small downtown stretch was one of the Eastside's most developed and lively areas. It was there that some of Puget Sound's biggest July Fourth celebrations were held, drawing throngs of onlookers. Mardi Gras festivities were also held there, an idea that started as a fund-raiser to pay for a firetruck.

"Woodinville didn't have a main street, a center core. Kenmore didn't have that circle where you could say this was downtown," said Sue Kienast of the Bothell Historical Museum. "So this was where the people and the merchants were. It had a sense of community."

It was a community that no fire could take away. The dry timbers that made up the Main Street store fronts became breeding grounds for fire. But the town folks always rebuilt, even after the Great Fire of 1911 burned all 11 buildings on Easter morning.

By the 1920s, brick buildings brought a new look and permanence to downtown, ending the constant fire threat. And brick roads brought more travelers to town. Traveling would never be the same again.

The railroad laid by the river in the late 1890s became a secondary mode of transportation, and the steamboats that brought the settlers here became obsolete. Gone, too, was the logging industry, fading slowly at the turn of the century as the open land became farm land.

Farming gave Main and adjacent streets poultry men and dairy farmers, produce stands and grocery stores. It made Bothell a self-sustaining city in the 1910s, a city that historian Kienast said, "had all the amenities that everyone needed."

So more folks came. The doctors, merchants and lawyers pushed the farmers farther east in the valley until there was no more farmland left.

"We had the chicken farmers and the dairy farmers until the 1950s and 1960s," said former Mayor Bud Ericksen, whose grandfather was among the first settlers. "Then the residential situation became more prevalent."

A bedroom community

The flood of newcomers in the post-World War II years turned Bothell into a bedroom community, expanding the city to the north and west.

The river that once carried the early settlers and their logs downriver became a playground for new residents. Beginning in the 1940s, boat races were held every April, with cars parked along the roads from Kenmore to Woodinville and people lining the riverbanks and the 102nd Avenue bridge to watch.

The races continued until 1975, stopping after townsfolk protested against the potential hazard to competitors and the environment.

The big trees were long gone, but in 1962 local residents celebrated when a giant 112-foot fir at Main Street and 102nd Street was declared "the world's largest living Christmas tree" by Life magazine. The top of the tree eventually withered and was cut off.

Sources include "Squak Slough 1870-1920" by Amy Eunice Stickney and Lucile McDonald; "Slough of Memories," compiled by Fred Klein and the Northshore History Boosters; and "Little History of Bothell, Washington" by Jack R. Evans.

OFFBEAT MOMENTS IN BOTHELL HISTORY

In October 1886, Democratic District Attorney J.T. Ronald won all 38 Republican votes in Bothell after a campaign speech in which he had to introduce himself because there was no other Democrat in town to do it. Later, George Bothell, the Republican precinct leader, told him, "Here I thought I'd (give) you a complimentary vote so you'd have at least one ballot in your favor. Every other Republican . . . had the same idea."

Charles V. Beardslee, a teacher at Bothell and North Creek schools in the 1890s, allowed students to go fishing during recess. A colorful personality, he was justice of the peace and a founder of the Bothell State Bank. He also started the Bothell Cornet Band, a top city attraction in the 1900s.

UNDATED PHOTO

To celebrate Norway Day in 1909, Scandinavian locals built a Viking ship with a sea-serpent prow and a tail on the stern. Decked out in Viking attire, they rowed down Lake Washington and into the Alaska-Yukon-Pacific Exposition.

In May 1912, S.F. Woody, who later became mayor, was accused of speeding across the Bothell bridge at 12 mph. Woody got the case dismissed on grounds of insufficient evidence.

In 1944, Joe Ryan got elected mayor under the premise that he would paint the fireplugs white so "the dogs would have a better shot."

During the 1960s, a developer built a post office on Beardslee Boulevard in the wrong place. The building crossed over the line of another property owner, and the builder had to buy the land to square the deal.

CHAPTER 6

PEWS AND PULPITS

As settlers arrive, so do circuit-riding preachers and log-cabin congregations

Settlers on the Eastside got religion early. Circuit-riding preachers appeared almost as soon as the first pioneers, and prayer meetings were a regular occurrence in local school houses and log-cabin homes long before the first churches appeared.

By 1879, three local churches were well-established. The first two were built between 1873 and 1874 in the coal-mining town of Newcastle. One was the St. Cyprian Catholic Church. The other was more unusual: the 150-seat, nondenominational Sunday School Church, organized and built by the miners who were reputed to be a rough-and-tumble bunch.

The third church, originally located across from today's Marsh Park in Kirkland, grew out of unexpected company at Caroline and Sam French's home in 1879. Samuel Greene and a Rev. Harrison arrived as the French family, including adult son Harry, was sitting down to dinner one evening. Harrison and Greene were on a mission trip from Seattle and wanted to start a Sunday School east of Lake Washington.

Harry French volunteered his cabin for the weekly services and later donated the land for the First Church of Christ at Pleasant Bay. (The former name of Yarrow Bay.)

Well-established Eastern church congregations typically supported new or mission churches in the West, and the fledgling Kirkland church was twice-blessed. The Central Congregational Church of Providence, R.I., donated $100 to the new church — enough to purchase pews and a pulpit. (The weekly collection at the Frenchs' Sunday school was $2 to $3.)

It also received a bell from Sarah Jane Houghton of

BOTHELL HISTORICAL SOCIETY

The Rev. Samuel Greene

Boston, who had it made and shipped to Seattle because there was no foundry on the West Coast that made bells. Later, when the U.S. Postal Service wanted to change the name of Pleasant Bay, Caroline French suggested the community be called Houghton, in honor of the Boston benefactor.

Although the church has changed names, moved and been rebuilt, the bell remains an important part of Kirkland Congregational Church, now located near today's City Hall.

Building new churches

Because settlements were farspread and travel was difficult, other Eastside churches weren't far behind the original three.

By 1892, 40-50 people of diverse Christian denominations were gathering each Sunday afternoon in

The First Lutheran Church in Bothell, built in 1887 at the corner of Second and Fir streets, was moved a few feet in 1921. The congregation poses on the church's steps in 1948.

BY SHERRY GRINDELAND

Bellevue for the Union Sunday School. Two dozen of those people organized First Congregational Church in 1896, building on the corner of today's Northeast Eighth Street and 108th Avenue Northeast. The wood for what was called The Little White Church was shipped from Seattle. Volunteers shingled the roof but refused to do the belfry because it was too high.

Finally, a young man, 17-year-old Holly Ivey, climbed up with hammer in hand and did the job.

One of the original Bothell settlers, Columbus Greenleaf, opened his home to the Norwegian Lutherans and other prayer groups for services in 1870. The prayer groups eventually formed Bothell's First Lutheran Church and the Methodist Episcopal Church, both organized in the late 1880s.

Keeping the churches operating was a challenge. There was a national financial recession in the early 1890s, and Bothell's First Lutheran board minutes from 1893 contained these terse lines: "Times hard. Real struggle." In 1894, the board rented the building to other churches for $1 per meeting to bring in needed cash.

Although the church was on more solid financial footing by 1914, the ground wasn't as secure. That year, Second Street in front of the church was graded, and suddenly passing traffic made the building shiver and shake. A retaining wall was erected around the church, but by 1921 the building was obviously in trouble and both the church and parsonage were moved back several feet.

The stuff of legends

Interesting tales about early churches and pastors

abound.

• One circuit preacher, for example, made a deal with Issaquah's baseball team in 1894. If they would attend his church services on Sunday mornings, he would go to their baseball games on Sunday afternoons.

• Issaquah's original Methodist church, built in 1890, sat on cinder blocks. Hogs moved into the space under the church and disrupted evening services with noises and smells.

The enterprising minister hammered boards in place to block their entry. Then people complained about the location of the church, saying it would be better if it were moved a few feet. A wind storm blew the church off the blocks, moving it exactly to the location people had wanted, but smashed all the windows and toppled the chimney in the process.

• The Rev. Rosine Edwards was the Eastside's first female pastor, presiding from 1899-1900 at Tolt Congregational Church. When she finished church services in town, she walked three miles to Healy Logging Camp in Stillwater to conduct afternoon services.

• Another roving preacher was the Rev. A.J. McNamee, who in 1885 spent three weeks riding his circuit. He started in Seattle, stopped at Meydenbauer Bay, then at the Northup family home in Houghton, held services in the ballroom above George Tibbetts' store in Squak (Issaquah), and then went to Fall City and Tolt.

The role of women

Churches were clearly important to the small, developing communities.

This Sunday School Church class in Newcastle reflects the diversity of the mining community.

RENTON HISTORICAL SOCIETY

The Sunday School Church in Newcastle, shown in this late 1890s photo, was built around 1873.

"Churches connoted family, stability and community," said University of Washington history professor John Findlay. According to Findlay, church-related activities provided the only respectable social outlet for women isolated on homesteads.

Sunday schools for adults and children often predated churches because women could organize them with just a few people. Churches, on the other hand, required a dozen or more families and their cash donations to operate.

Women's church groups, often called Ladies Aid Societies, were more than mere coffee klatches. At First Lutheran in Bothell, one ladies group raised enough money to build the first parish hall in 1931 and another added a kitchen in 1935.

In North Bend the Ladies Aid Society made and sold pillow cases and aprons and held suppers and box socials, making enough money to build a room for the Sunday school, revarnish the church seats and woodwork and pay for a plank sidewalk that ran from the business district to the church.

Spiritual roots

Most early churches on the Eastside were mainstream Christian. At least one was segregated. A photograph from the 1890s shows the congregation of a black church in Kennydale.

Although there were Chinese workers in both Issaquah and Newcastle in the late 1880s, there are no records of their religious practices. The Mormons were established in Seattle in 1902, and in 1937 two Kirkland women convinced LDS leaders to start a local Sunday School. In 1969, the first Jewish services were held on Mercer Island. The Islamic Center of the Eastside in Bellevue opened in 1996, and a Buddhist temple opened in Redmond in 1985.

Spiritual roots, however, have run deep on the Eastside for centuries. Local Native American tribes, including the Snoqualmie, revered a natural world they believed was filled with spirits. Many Snoqualmie tribal members joined the Shaker Church, but prior to that local tribes used community longhouses for religious ceremonies.

"Churches always were a sign of stability and a gathering place for isolated settlers," said Trudy Eichelsdoerfer of Bothell, who wrote the history of Bothell's First Lutheran Church. "Even today they're considered a cornerstone of our local communities."

Sources: "Our Foundering Fathers," by Arline Ely; "Coals to Newcastle" by Richard McDonald and Lucile McDonald; Issaquah Historical Society; Renton Historical Society; the Eastside Heritage Society's Marymoor Museum; The Seattle Times; archives from First Lutheran Church of Bothell, First Congregational Church of Bellevue and the Congregational Church of Kirkland.

Ladies Aid Societies were instrumental in raising money for church projects. Here a group from the First Congregational Church of Bellevue meets at the home of R.G. Macdonald.

FIRST CONGREGATIONAL CHURCH, BELLEVUE

CHAPTER 7

WOMEN OF CHANGE

They made an impact on the Eastside well before winning the right to vote

From the beginning, Eastside women preached, ran businesses and governed communities. Long before it was taken for granted that women would, these pioneers ventured outside the sphere of domesticity and left their imprint on the larger community.

There was Susan Woodin, whose home held the first church, school and post office in what later became Woodinville, named for her family. In Bellevue, Isabel Bechtel served as postmistress, taking on the duties of her husband in 1891 after he was killed in a logjam.

Kirkland's Eliza Forbes became King County's first female justice of the peace in 1887 — only to have her office rescinded when Washington became a state in 1889. At the same time in Newcastle, Georgianna Fournier Rouse traveled to miners' houses to deliver babies and provide health care as the community's midwife.

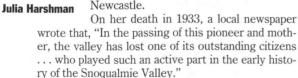

Eliza Forbes

The Eastside's history is dotted with stories of these and countless other women who, by chance or personal ambition, found themselves in the forefront of change.

SEATTLE TIMES ARCHIVES

JULIA HARSHMAN

Telephone-company pioneer

It would be difficult to underestimate the effect of Julia Harshman's business on the Snoqualmie Valley. In 1903, she and her husband moved to Fall City, where he operated a sawmill with another local man. To keep in touch with their families, the men set up a phone line between their houses and the mill.

Neighbors soon began asking to be hooked up; and by 1907, Julia was operating a switchboard in her house for The Fall City Telephone Co. When her husband died in 1929, she took over the business, which had grown to 300 phones, linking Fall City, Carnation, Preston, North Bend, Snoqualmie and Newcastle.

Julia Harshman

On her death in 1933, a local newspaper wrote that, "In the passing of this pioneer and mother, the valley has lost one of its outstanding citizens . . . who played such an active part in the early history of the Snoqualmie Valley."

NELLIE CLARKE STIMSON

Farsighted entrepreneur

Nellie Clarke Stimson's Woodinville business reached beyond the Eastside, beyond even the United States mainland. The flowers she grew at Hollywood Gardens were shipped as far as Honolulu and Nome, Alaska.

She opened the greenhouses of Hollywood Gardens soon after her husband built their lavish country home in 1910; and the business she ran fast became one of the Northwest's biggest floral growing and delivery services.

The iron and concrete greenhouses with their oil-fired steam heating plant were said to be the most modern of any west of the Mississippi.

Historians believe she also designed the beautifully landscaped grounds, which were once thought to be the handiwork of the renowned Olmsted brothers, designers of many Seattle parks. The Chateau Ste. Michelle winery now sits on the land.

Stimson sold the home in 1927, but the site of Hollywood Gardens is memorialized with listings on both the King County and National Registers of Historic Places.

Postmistress Isabel Bechtel and daughters Maude and Jessie are photographed about 1900 in front of their log cabin, which was Bellevue's second post office.

BY JANET BURKITT

THE REV. ROSINE EDWARDS
Pastor to loggers

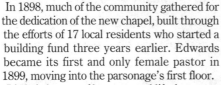

Rosine Edwards

The wood-frame Tolt Congregational Church where the Rev. Rosine Edwards once preached burned in 1936, but stories of her dedication still reverberate in the pews of the stone church now standing in Carnation.

In 1898, much of the community gathered for the dedication of the new chapel, built through the efforts of 17 local residents who started a building fund three years earlier. Edwards became its first and only female pastor in 1899, moving into the parsonage's first floor.

Little is known of her personal life, but more is known of her dedication to the church. On Sundays, Edwards walked several miles over hills and through forests to the Healy Logging Camp at Stillwater "to bring her sincere message to the men in the woods," according to church records.

"This work alone proves what strength she had in her conviction and what courage she had to carry it through, even though she was just a young woman."

LUCINDA FARES
First white female settler

The Snoqualmie Valley was a much wilder place when Lucinda Fares moved there in 1860, becoming its first white female settler and its first dairy farmer.

But Fares already was used to the frontier: She came west with her parents nine years earlier to homestead by the Duwamish River, which made her and her mother the first white women in King County as well.

Though she couldn't read or write, she learned to speak the languages of the Duwamish and Snoqualmie Indians, knowledge that made her a hero when she was still a girl. She rescued her neighbor, Henry Van Asselt, from what historian Mildred Tanner Andrews describes as "almost certain massacre" by talking to an armed group of Native Americans.

She told them about a lead shot embedded in his arm, knowing that that made him invincible in the belief system of the Duwamish Indians.

CARRIE SHUMWAY
State's first councilwoman

In 1911, a year after women won the vote in Washington, Kirkland voters made Carrie Shumway the first city councilwoman in the state. She had just returned from teaching English in Tokyo and had little interest in politics, but her fellow Kirklanders persuaded her to tackle the job.

Shumway and her four sisters were already leaders in the community, founding the Seattle Bicycle Club and the Seattle Camera Club. She was one of the first teachers in the Seattle Public School system, a founding member of the Kirkland Women's Club and state historian for the Daughters of the American Revolution.

As the last surviving member of her family, Shumway sold the 18-room family mansion. The New England-style home is still preserved in Kirkland.

Sources include "Woman's Place: A Guide to Seattle and King County History" by Mildred Tanner Andrews.

BURROWS COLLECTION/BELLEVUE HISTORICAL SOCIETY

META JACOBSON BURROWS
Influential business owner

Burrows' Lakeside Drug Store, shown here in probably the 1940s, was a community hub.

When Meta Jacobson Burrows earned a pharmacology degree from the University of Washington in 1934 — one of about a dozen women who graduated that year — her father's graduation gift was a partnership in Bellevue's Lakeside Drug Store. By the end of the year, Burrows owned the shop.

She joined the Chamber of Commerce and attended Business Men's Association meetings. Soon businessmen were holding informal sessions at her soda fountain, a place where "many community projects germinated over coffee and cinnamon rolls," according to Eastside historian Lucile McDonald.

Burrows continued running the store after she married a local butcher-shop owner.

When she finally did close Lakeside Drug Store in 1979, it was Bellevue's oldest continually operating business.

STELLA ALEXANDER
Strong-willed mayor

The Great Depression paved the way for later strong-headed women with political aspirations. Issaquah voters liked Stella Alexander's promise to lower the cost of new sidewalks for taxpayers and, in 1932, chose her as the city's first woman mayor.

But some City Council members were not quite so progressive as those they represented. Three of them refused to serve under a woman, so Alexander appointed replacements — without the legal authority to do so.

When two sets of council members appeared at the next council meeting, she made a motion to have one group leave. No one supported that motion, so she made a physical one — aiming an oak chair at one of the councilmen. "The mayor was a fairly large and strong woman," wrote Issaquah historian Joe Peterson.

Her volatility didn't set well with voters: They petitioned for a recall election and voted her out in 1934.

Stella Alexander

CHAPTER 8

THE OLD SCHOOLS

Frontier students waded through mud and endured the whip for an education

ISABEL JONES

At the Tolt School, shown here in 1909, students learned to read using the phonics method.

The Eastside's first schoolteachers were a colorful lot who didn't spare the rod. Ruffian children of loggers and homesteaders frequently tried to run weak teachers out of the classroom in a test of wills. The teachers, often teenagers themselves with no college education, demanded obedience.

Old-timers' accounts of schools a century ago mention little about their lessons but recall the punishments well.

"My greatest horror of getting whipped in school was thinking of the loss of respect and hurt feelings my parents would undergo when they would find it out," says a memoir by the late Elmer Carlberg, who attended the Derby School at the turn of the century in what is now Woodinville. The school later became the Hollywood School.

"My older sister told me about seeing a classmate getting choked so hard by the teacher he was getting blue in the face. This frightened the rest of the chil-

dren and made them cry, and made the teacher release his hold. But there are humorous sides to this corporal punishment: Sister told me of a girl classmate who got her mouth washed out with soap and water for lying."

In 1890, Bothell boys and girls fought so fiercely that the girls grabbed sticks and clubs until teacher Charles Beardsley separated the groups.

An early teaching legend was Homer Turner, hired in 1887 at age 17. He quit five months later to take long-shore work, then returned in the mid-1890s. Early in his career, he whacked the largest boy in the head with a curtain rod to quell a classroom rebellion. To keep children from being distracted, he covered the windows.

BY MIKE LINDBLOM

The school wagon pictured here took children to the Tolt School in Carnation. The photo was taken between 1900 and 1910.

ISABEL JONES

"Homer Turner drove them like oxen, he held the club over them so much," one early account reports. "He would walk among them tapping them on their shoulders, and he had a trick of snapping a pencil clear across a large schoolroom and always getting his mark on some youngster's head."

Turner was also known for his brilliance: He was the first Bothell teacher to present material above the eighth-grade level.

Surmounting hardships

Parents, teachers and children had to surmount hardships just to conduct classes.

North Bend-area landowners founded schools in ranch cabins during the 1880s. They hired a few odd characters. A squatter named Asa Storey found a job teaching even though he "did not like civilization and avoided close neighbors," a history of the area says.

His successor, lacking education himself, insisted that three times zero was three. Students walked out on him.

Woodinville's first classes, in 1881, took place inside town founder Ira Woodin's family home along the Sammamish Slough. Students from Bothell walked through mud to get there until their school was finished a few years later.

The first Bellevue school, in 1883, was built along what is now Meydenbauer Bay by parent Albert Burrows, who made the desks and three blackboards. His daughter, Calanthia, was the first teacher of Killarney School, which her two brothers and five others attended.

Mercer Island's first school opened in a shanty the next year. The two schools alternated their teaching seasons, so children rowed and sometimes swam across the East Channel of Lake Washington to attend classes. The Burrows' family dog, Judge, carried the boys' lunch box across the lake in his teeth.

Students along the Snoqualmie River in both the Carnation and North Bend areas likewise traveled in canoes or rafts to school.

In 1892, the Mercer Slough School opened in an

REVISITING THE OLD SCHOOLS

Several old Eastside schools still stand. Some examples:

Bothell School (1885) has been restored, furnished with century-old desks and books, and moved from its original site on downtown's Main Street to Bothell Landing Park for public viewing.

North Creek School (1897), a fading-white, one-room school, still sits, though neglected and deteriorating, at 228th Street Southeast and 33rd Avenue East in the Canyon Park area of Bothell.

High Point School (1903) has become Trinity Evangelical Church. It sits at the end of Southeast 76th Place just north of the High Point Road exit along Interstate 90 in Issaquah.

Vincent School (1905), an old elementary school west of Carnation, is now a community

center. The address is 8001 W. Snoqualmie Valley Road N.E., near the Nestle Training Center.

Hollywood School (1912) is now a community center on the northeast corner of Northeast 145th Street and Woodinville-Redmond Road in Woodinville.

Redmond School (1922) is now a parks-department building and community center just north of downtown Redmond at 16600 N.E. 80th St. A new Redmond Elementary opened next door in the fall of 1998.

abandoned bachelor's cabin with shake roofing and a woodstove.

"The cracks between the floorboards were so wide the skunks used to come up and look for crumbs when we ate our lunch," recalls pupil Helen Thode Boddy in Lucile McDonald's book "Bellevue: The First 100 Years."

"We had no (outhouse), so the boys went to the woods on one side and the girls on the other. Our teacher was very much afraid of bears."

Bellevue's tradition of parent involvement started early this century. The weekly Lake Washington Reflector reported on PTA meetings, where school choirs and orchestras regularly performed.

A guest speaker in 1928 complained that "much school time is wasted in activities outside the original three R's, and the present apparent aim of many students is to get credits regardless of knowledge."

Hooked on phonics

Around 1900, a pedagogical fashion called phonics swept the Eastside along with the rest of the country. Issaquah-area schools used the New Education Readers, which taught reading through mastery of consonant and vowel sounds. A drawing of a hissing cat illustrated the "f-f-f" sound, while a blacksmith's sizzling horseshoe produced "s-s-s."

"They had little cards with all the syllables, and you put it together," remembers Wes Larson, who attended Tolt School in Carnation in the 1920s.

Strict teaching styles survived into the relatively freewheeling 1920s. Redmond student Lester Olson remembers the feeling of being slapped in the open palm with a ruler when he attended the new brick school downtown.

A fourth-grade teacher mocked Olson, whose family spoke Swedish at home, for not knowing the English word "astonished," he recalls.

Olson still lives in an old family home along Redmond-Fall City Road Northeast. Recently he visited Lake Washington School District's Alcott Elementary, which his great-grandson Dillon Nelson attends.

The school provides computers and keeps teacher-student ratios far below the 50 children per room of Olson's time. And students aren't getting whacked.

"There's no resemblance at all," Olson says. "It was just so completely different. It wasn't like a school."

ISABEL JONES

The Pleasant Hill School in Carnation was the site of this church gathering in 1902.

A page from the New Education Reader, a 1900 phonics textbook used in Issaquah schools.

Sources include "A History of Snoqualmie Valley" by Ada Snyder Hill, "Redmond: Our Town" by Nancy Way, "Bellevue: The First 100 Years" by Lucile McDonald, "A History of Tolt/Carnation" by Isabel L. Jones, back editions of The Bothell Citizen and scrapbook materials from the Bellevue Historical Society.

CHAPTER 9

SNOQUALMIE

Expansive prairie became home to farms, power plant, lumber mill

The view from the train depot in Snoqualmie shows Main Street on a snowy April morning. Mount Si is in the background.

SNOQUALMIE VALLEY HISTORICAL SOCIETY, 1911

In the hours before dusk, elk travel down Rattlesnake Ridge to graze in the meadows on Snoqualmie's edge. Coyotes lope after them, almost silly in their attempts to stalk more-powerful prey.

Mount Si looms to the south, the closest link in a circle of tree-lined stones. Ignore the blackberry brambles, an invasive species introduced in the 1880s, and you can almost picture what the land looked like in the days before highways and housing developments turned Snoqualmie into one of the Eastside's fastest-growing cities.

Meadowbrook Farm, a 453-acre open-space preserve, is what's left of an expansive prairie that once covered the valley floor.

This place, where people park their cars to watch wildlife appear and disappear among the trees, is a visual reminder of the abundance that sustained generations of Native Americans and, later, attracted white newcomers who transformed a backwater settlement into an economic center in the first half of the 20th century.

For at least 5,000 years, the people who would come to be called Snoqualmie Indians set fires to maintain the open prairie. The periodic burning of the land encouraged berries and edible-root plants to grow and lured elk, black-tail deer

BY SARA JEAN GREEN

SNOQUALMIE VALLEY HISTORICAL SOCIETY, 1919

and other game to forage in the open fields.

"It probably looks more like it did now than at any time since the first white settlers showed up in the valley," said Dave Battey, a longtime resident and Snoqualmie's unofficial historian.

Across Southeast Park Street from Mount Si High School's playing fields, there's now a trailer park at the site where militia soldiers — the first white residents in the valley — built Fort Alden in 1856.

It was one in a series of forts built in the Snoqualmie Valley during the Indian War of 1856 because of fears Native Americans from east of the Cascades would join coastal tribes, angry with the terms of the Point Elliott Treaty signed the year before. An attack never came, and the fort was abandoned.

Soon after, Jeremiah Borst arrived on the Snoqualmie Prairie. Using the old fort as his cabin, he began farming, eventually owning 900 acres, including the entire Meadowbrook area. He planted an orchard and raised hogs, transporting his meat and produce to Everett for sale in Seattle. Borst, who married into the family of Snoqualmie chief Patkanim, is often called "The Father of the Snoqualmie Valley." He was the valley's first postmaster, paid the first teacher's salary so his children could go to school, helped establish the first wagon road across Snoqualmie Pass in the 1860s and

served two terms as county commissioner in the 1870s.

A barn and blacksmith shop were erected at the Fort Alden site after Borst sold most of his property — for $12.50 per acre — to the Hop Growers' Association in 1882.

Founded by three Puget Sound partners, the Snoqualmie Hop Farm was billed as the largest hop ranch in the world. Hop vines and fruit orchards covered 1,500 acres and employed hundreds of people, including European settlers and Native Americans from Yakima up to the Frasier River basin in British Columbia.

By the late 1890s, the hop market had crashed and an insect infestation all but wiped out the Snoqualmie crops. In the early 1900s, the Hop Farm became Meadowbrook Farm, a large cattle and dairy operation that continued into the 1950s.

Railroads and rivalry

Snoqualmie's population was spurred by logging operations that employed 140 men by 1886 and the coming of the railroad in 1889. With the trains came feverish speculation in Upper Snoqualmie Valley land, sparking the rivalry between Snoqualmie and its neighbor, North Bend, that lasted until the two cities merged their high schools — and their hometown teams — in the mid-1940s.

Edmund and Louisa Kinsey and their six children came to be known as Snoqualmie's "first family."

SNOQUALMIE VALLEY HISTORICAL SOCIETY

The Snoqualmie Falls Lumber Co., which opened in 1917, was the nation's second all-electric mill. The company would later become Weyerhaeuser.

The rivalry dates to the early 1890s, when North Bend was called Snoqualmie and Snoqualmie was called Snoqualmie Falls. What is now Snoqualmie got its name — and the railway depot that was originally slated to go to North Bend — by wooing railway officials when North Bend's founder (land speculator Will Taylor, who platted the city) was out of town.

To avoid confusion, railroad officials created rules against nearby towns sharing similar names and so "forced (what is now) North Bend to change its name and made Snoqualmie Falls drop 'Falls'" from the town's moniker, said Battey.

The railroad depot, on Railroad Avenue in Snoqualmie's old downtown core, soon attracted other business interests to the city. Edmund and Louisa Kinsey, who are believed to have purchased the first lots in the new town, quickly became community stalwarts. The couple and their six children are widely considered Snoqualmie's "first Family."

"In the 1890s, they provided newborn Snoqualmie with a hotel, store, post office, church, meat market and community center," reads the inscription on a plaque commemorating the Kinsey family that hangs outside the 1923 building that housed the town's first bank. (The building was used as a city hall until the 1990 flood forced city staff into a newer building).

According to Battey, the Kinsey family was also responsible for building the town's first livery stable and a hall for the Good Templars, "an amazingly strong political force" that influenced the national prohibition movement. Two of the Kinsey sons — Darius and Clarke — went on to regional fame photographing logging camps and farming operations.

Company town

Newcomers flooded into Snoqualmie after an underground power plant was built at Snoqualmie Falls in the late 1890s, producing electricity and local jobs. A small company town, including a railroad depot, grew up around the falls. A second powerhouse was

added in 1911.

A few years later, in 1917, the Snoqualmie Falls Lumber Co. cut its first log. The owners of the second all-electric lumber mill in the country built their own company town — called Snoqualmie Falls—across the river and up a hill from Snoqualmie. At its peak, the mill town included 250 homes, a hotel, community center, 50-bed hospital, barber shop, grade school, boarding house for single men and eight bunkhouses built for Japanese workers.

During World War I, soldiers were assigned to the mill and woods so that wood, an essential material for

Mill No. 1 of the Snoqualmie Falls Lumber Co. cut its first log on Nov. 25, 1917. The sawmill had an 11-foot headrig to cut Douglas fir.

This Darius Kinsey photo was taken during World War I when the mill began employing women. Kinsey and his brother, Clarke, photographed logging camps and farming operations in the Northwest.

A Snoqualmie Falls house is moved across a temporary bridge to Snoqualmie to its new location in the Williams Addition. The bridge was torn down shortly thereafter.

the war effort, could still be logged and processed.

Though mill wages fell through the Great Depression, the Snoqualmie Falls Lumber Co. — which later became Weyerhaeuser — survived the hard times to enjoy the nation's post-World War II building boom that increased demand for lumber.

By the 1950s, the idea of a mill town had fallen out of vogue. The houses at Snoqualmie Falls were in need of expensive maintenance and mill workers, who rented from the company, wanted the chance to own their own homes. Many of the houses were moved across a temporary bridge on the Snoqualmie River to create the Williams Addition to Snoqualmie in 1958.

By 1960, Snoqualmie's population had stabilized at around 1,200 residents. By then, agriculture was no longer a major economic force in the community, but Weyerhaeuser's milling operations were still a mainstay. With the completion of Interstate 90 in the 1970s, more Snoqualmie residents began commuting to jobs outside the city. Still, over the next 30 years, only about 11 people were added to the city's rolls each year.

In 1989, Weyerhaeuser closed its main mill above Snoqualmie. In 2002, the company announced it was shutting down its Snoqualmie dry kilns and planing plant. The closure, along with Weyerhaeuser's decision to mothball its White River mill in Enumclaw, effectively ended the company's 100-year logging operation in King County.

A new chapter in Snoqualmie's history began in 1990 when the city annexed 1,300 acres of Weyerhaeuser land on a ridge northwest of the city. Since the first houses in the Snoqualmie Ridge development were completed in 1996, the city has grown to a population of 4,600. With a second Ridge project planned and other housing developments in the works, city officials project 8,000 people will live in Snoqualmie by 2014.

Sources include: "28 Historic Places in the Upper Snoqualmie Valley," by Kenneth G. (Greg) Watson, Snoqualmie Valley Historical Museum, 1992; "Meadowbrook Farm Master Site Plan," prepared by RCA Huitt-Zollars & Meadowbrook Farm Preservation Association, Adopted by the cities of Snoqualmie and North Bend, 1999; www.cityofsnoqualmie.net; "A Short History of the Upper Snoqualmie Valley," by Dave Battey, Snoqualmie Valley Historical Society, www.snovalley.org/vl_history.html.

CHAPTER 10

HOPS AND DREAMS

A short-lived boom in the 1880s left a long legacy in the Snoqualmie Valley

When people think of the North-west hops industry, the sunny Yakima Valley comes to mind. But more than a century ago it was the state's wet side that grew a world-famous crop known as "cluster gold."

The Snoqualmie Valley was home to a hop craze in the 1880s that promised quick profits for settlers and employed tribal members who were being displaced from their land.

The boom started in 1881, when a European hop blight threatened Britain's ale supply, and growers here filled the void. For homesteaders who were clearing their land, hops were an ideal cash crop because they yielded a crop the first year. At the industry's peak, export-grade hops earned an astounding $1 per pound.

In the shadow of Mount Si, settlers formed the Snoqualmie Hop Ranch, a 1,200-acre expanse of woods, orchards and gardens that included 450 acres of hop rows.

A three-story hotel on the site attracted tourists from Boston, San Francisco and Seattle who watched the September spectacle of a thousand workers, mostly Native Americans, stripping cones off the vines.

The industry collapsed in the 1890s. Today only a few artifacts remain, the most visible being George Davis Rutherford's hop-drying kiln in Fall City — the last of 80 kilns in the area.

"It marks a transition into the agricultural era in the Snoqualmie Valley," said Allen Minner, a leader in the hop shed preservation group. "After the hops craze in the valley, what else was there?"

An essential crop

Greg Watson, director of the Snoqualmie Valley Historical Museum, believes hop plants first reached the Northwest on British ships of the Hudson's Bay Co., which traded at Fort Nisqually in 1833 and on the Columbia River before that.

"It's hard to imagine any Englishmen coming out

here without the means to produce beer," he said. Without hops, which impart a snappy, bitter flavor, beer would taste like soggy bread.

In 1865 entrepreneur Ezra Meeker planted a large hop farm in Puyallup and taught other settlers to do likewise.

Fields soon reached as far north as Issaquah, and Kent was named for England's scenic hop-growing region. England bought most of the crop, though Meeker's clients included Oregon brewer Henry Weinhard.

The state Board of Horticulture bragged that at 1,327 pounds per acre, Washington hop farms in 1892

Most pickers were members of the Snoqualmie Tribe, usually women. This photo was taken around 1890.

By Mike Lindblom

were twice as productive as those in England or Germany.

But the most important effect of hop commerce in the Snoqualmie Valley wasn't the small fortune a few people earned, rather the means it provided displaced Native American families "to 'hang on' during a period of social and economic change," writes Kenneth Tollefson, a retired Seattle Pacific University anthropologist.

Singing in the fields

Hop pickers wore straw hats as sun shields and brass badges printed with their payroll numbers. Most were Snoqualmie tribal members, but there were also many white homesteaders who needed cash. Other Natives canoed in from as far away as British Columbia.

"Hop pole!" they'd yell, as a man would wrestle a 10-foot hop pole with vines attached out of the dirt, laying it against an X-shape frame so women and children could reach the cones.

One adult could usually fill a 100-pound bin or two per day, earning about $1.

Children worked the fields at age 5 alongside their extended families.

Women carried infants on their backs in wooden cradleboards, with sticks extending down from the bottom that allowed the cradleboards to be set on the ground so mothers could easily squat and nurse babies without disrupting the work routine.

Sometimes they would hang cradleboards from trees. Men carried loads, picked or worked as hunting and fishing guides.

Natives insisted on being paid in silver dollars because they didn't trust paper money. The income went for modern needs such as flour and knives, as well as to gambling. The Snoqualmies' weekend horse races also attracted white tourists.

Naturalist John Muir wrote after an 1890 visit, "About a thousand Indians are required as pickers at the Snoqualmie Ranch alone, and a lively and merry picture they make in the field, arrayed in bright, showy calicoes, lowering the rustling vine-pillars with incessant song-singing and fun."

The Snoqualmies, who had just become landless refugees, lived a "semi-subsistence" lifestyle that required money to supplement other resources such as salmon and gardening. In turn, whites relied on their labor.

Unlike other Native Americans, the Snoqualmies tied and cultivated hops several months a year because they lived in the area.

The tribe established a village along Lake Sammamish, in "shacks and hovels at the head of the lake," an Issaquah writer said.

They'd leave for the hop fields for four to six weeks at a time. Migrating Native workers carried woven mats throughout the county for a source of portable shelter.

A boatload of 37 Chinese arrived in Issaquah in the early 1870s willing to work for lower wages and provoked resentment among local pickers. A group of five whites and two Snoqualmies fired into Chinese tents at night, killing three and wounding three.

Workers at the Snoqualmie Hop Ranch pose with an empty 100-pound bin in this 1893 photo. The ranch employed hundreds at harvest time.

Lice invade

In 1892 the tiny hop louse invaded Washington, Oregon and British Columbia. A female could produce a trillion descendants in one summer, and one photo shows 1,000 lice on a single leaf, sucking out the moisture.

The most effective treatment was a mixture of whale oil and South American quassia-tree bark that Meeker invented, but it was used inconsistently.

At the same time, European fields recovered, and world markets were glutted, driving the price down.

George Davis Rutherford, a small farmer in Fall City, made only 11 cents a pound for one of his 1893 shipments to New York, according to records that his granddaughter Maryln Everett Hunt still keeps in a home closet. That amounted to $613 for 28 bales, apparently one-fourth of the previous year's harvest. It all went to shipping fees and paying off debts. Some years he sold off land to stay solvent.

Under such conditions, hops practically disappeared from the area by the turn of the century. The Snoqualmie Hop Ranch, Rutherford farm and most others reverted to food crops.

But hops still thrived in the Yakima Valley, where hot weather killed off lice. The Snoqualmies moved throughout the state picking berries and apples.

Some stubborn hop vines continue to grow at the original Snoqualmie Valley Ranch site. To preserve the living legacy, Watson transplanted some to the museum grounds and his Enumclaw home. He brews a strong amber ale that could have passed for a British pub drink a century ago.

Sources include Rutherford family records; documents from the Fall City Hop Shed Foundation; "Ventures and Adventures of Ezra Meeker" by Ezra Meeker; Snoqualmie Valley Record newspaper articles; "The Snoqualmie Indians as Hop Pickers" by Kenneth Tollefson; and "Columbia," a journal of the Washington State Historical Society, winter 1994-95.

HOW HOP KILNS WORKED

Hop-drying kilns were essential to keep the crop from turning moldy at sea.

The George Davis Rutherford kiln, built in 1888 at the confluence of the Raging and Snoqualmie rivers, followed the common Western Washington design.

Farmworkers or a horse-drawn cart carried freshly filled bins up a ramp, where the cones were tossed onto an elevated kiln floor at a 1- to 3-inch depth. The floor had gaps that were covered with burlap, allowing 140-degree heat to rise through the cones.

On the floor sat a woodstove, its flue curving overhead so warmth moved evenly. Some kilns were stoked through an outside chute, and farmers hired boys to keep the fires going overnight.

Rutherford's kiln was sold, moved and converted into a root cellar in 1904. A community group replaced the foundation and roof in 1997. The kiln can be viewed in Fall City Community Park, across the Snoqualmie River from downtown.

George Davis Rutherford

A magazine drawing shows how hops were dried and then shipped in 200-pound bales.

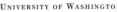

CHAPTER 11

ISSAQUAH

One man's industrial adventures shaped the Eastside's oldest city

Even as he was heading west, Gen. George Washington Tibbetts stopped midway through his trip to open a store and start a bank. When this mover and shaker settled in what is now Issaquah, his new home felt the full power of his entrepreneurial spirit — in everything from a cross-Cascade highway to a single can of milk.

George Tibbetts

The Eastside's oldest incorporated city was built on a combination of commerce, agriculture and location. Hops, dairy farms, mining and lumber were all big businesses for Issaquah, and its location, roughly halfway between the Cascades and Seattle, made it a stopping point on westward routes.

Behind development and innovations in nearly all these areas was Tibbetts — planning, growing, building and selling, and in the process helping to create a city.

The adventurous Maine native left home at age 16, heading west after serving in the Civil War. He stopped for a few years in Missouri, where he farmed, started a couple of businesses and married Rebecca Wilson.

The young couple homesteaded for a year in Oregon, where they lost two babies in two days, before moving to the Squak Valley in the early 1870s.

When they arrived, the fertile land between what are now Lake Sammamish and the Issaquah Alps was still a wild place. It was known then as Squak, a corruption of the Native American name for the area, Ishquoh. In 1870, the town had about 30 white residents.

Among these was one of Issaquah's most important settlers — William Pickering, a territorial governor appointed by Abraham Lincoln. The Tibbetts family stayed on Pickering's sprawling property while their home was being built.

Like Pickering, Tibbetts became active in early

Lars, Peter and Ingebright Wold established the hop-growing business in Issaquah in the late 1860s. In their hop houses, here circa 1895, the harvested plants were dried and baled.

SEATTLE TIMES ARCHIVES

BY JANET BURKITT

Families of Native American workers, as well as whites, joined in hop harvests. This photo probably was taken in the 1880s.

Washington government, serving as a territorial legislator in the 1870s and framer of the state constitution in the 1880s. As a state legislator, he drafted and pushed through a bill for a Snoqualmie Pass highway, the first over the Cascades.

Early industries

But these two were extraordinary in their pursuits: For most Squak pioneers at that time, life revolved around coal and hops, and Tibbetts soon became involved in the latter, buying plants from Puyallup's Ezra Meeker and growing them on his 160-acre ranch near Lake Sammamish.

At that time, hops farmers hired Native Americans and whites to pick the plants, which then were dried and baled in tall hop houses.

When Chinese laborers left Seattle to work in Squak hop fields, the local workers united to keep this new labor force out.

The whites and Indians chased away about 30 Chinese people at gunpoint before the workers even entered the valley, and killed and wounded others who had set up camp.

But neither the laborers nor the farm owners could do anything about the two forces that would destroy the business at the turn of the century: hop lice and Eastern Washington competition.

Tibbetts, however, continued to prosper. Along with the family home, Tibbetts had built a store, stage house and a hotel. These almost instantly became the commercial heart of the growing settlement, as well as its social center. Cross-Cascade travelers stayed overnight at the well-known "halfway house," and locals gathered to chat on the hotel's long porch and dance in its ballroom.

The kindness Tibbetts and his wife showed to travelers was legendary: During the winter, the couple sent wagons up the pass to make sure no one was stranded.

The hotel was popular mainly because it was a stop on the stage line Tibbetts established between Snoqualmie — where he built another store and a sawmill — and Newcastle, the "black diamond" capital of King County.

The line was essential to Issaquah's development, serving as a major means of ground trans-

portation before the railroad came to town.

In 1888, the year the railroad in Issaquah was completed, Tibbetts became Washington's representative to the national Republican convention. He also served locally, as postmaster in the mid-1870s and '80s.

Fortunately for him, he had stepped down by 1892, when the town's incorporation as Gilman led to lost mail.

The trouble was that there already was a Gilmer in Klickitat County, so Gilman adopted a different name — Olney — for its post office. The two names were a source of frustration for the townspeople in Gilman, who successfully petitioned Olympia for a name change. The city became Issaquah in 1899.

During these years, Tibbetts' retirement as postmaster seemed like the only thing that went right for him: The panic of 1893 wiped out most of his businesses and possessions.

Around 1900, a fire swept away Tibbetts' hotel and store on his ranch, just as local hops farming collapsed completely.

But Tibbetts, then about 55, recovered. He built yet another store, which soon was thriving. By then, Issaquah's commercial hub had shifted from his ranch to its present site on Front Street.

Issaquah's thriving downtown became centered along Front Street, pictured here in the 1930s.

From left: Issaquah Valley Dairy employees Bill Bergsma, Duane Murberg, an unidentified person, Gary Baugh, Steve Johnson and Marianne Boncutter. The school behind them was built in 1915.

ISSAQUAH HISTORICAL SOCIETY

Moving into milk

As usual, Tibbetts did not stop with only one venture. Logging came to Issaquah around 1903, and the old-growth trees that were cleared revealed excellent pastures for cows.

The dairy business took off. The Darigold creamery went up in 1909, and the Pickering family ran a dairy with the still-standing Pickering Barn as its centerpiece.

But it was Tibbetts who shipped the first can of milk from Issaquah to Seattle, establishing the little town as a major supplier to the big city. Soon, dairymen were loading up to 125 cans of milk each morning onto the train.

By the time Tibbetts died in 1924, many of the industries that had shaped Issaquah — hops, mining, lumber, dairy — were gone or on the decline. But the city had taken root.

Other innovators played key roles in founding Issaquah: Daniel Gilman brought the railroad; L.B. Andrews developed the first mine; W.W. Sylvester founded the Issaquah Bank.

But in a city put together from so many pieces, only Tibbetts seemed to have a hand in nearly all of them.

Today, he is regarded as the city's first entrepreneur and one of Washington's most esteemed pioneers.

Sources include "The History of King County" by Clarence Bagley, "The Past at Present in Issaquah, Washington" by Edwards Fish, "Fire Rock: The Story of Issaquah's Coal Mining History" by Linda Adair Hjelm, "This Was Issaquah," compiled by Harriet Fish, and the Issaquah Press archives.

CHAPTER 12

THE MELTING POT

Hard-working immigrants carve out a life on the Eastside

It was hardly Ellis Island West, but in its brief history the Eastside has been a surprising melting pot, home to a Babel of hard-working people who carved lives out of stubborn timber and bedrock.

Those who persevered formed the fabric of today's communities — communities that are now being embroidered by still more newcomers.

Immigrants often arrived in distinct waves, usually following the call of money, jobs or cheap land.

Before the first white settlers arrived in the 1860s, the area had long been home to the Snoqualmie and Duwamish, the Eastside's two main tribes.

The 4,000-strong Snoqualmies mostly occupied their namesake valley, while the Duwamish lived along the southern shores of Lake Washington around modern-day Renton.

In the years after the 1855 treaty that ceded Snoqualmie lands to the United States, some members moved to reservations (including Marysville's Tulalip Reservation), but many also stayed to work in white-owned industries, such as hop farming.

By 1870, so few whites lived east of Lake Washington that a single voting precinct extended from the Black River, near Renton, to the Bothell area.

A large percentage of those pioneers who arrived in

Erik Erickson and his sons and daughters pose at the High Point Saw Mill near today's Issaquah in 1910. The family had recently arrived from Sweden.

BY CHRIS SOLOMON

RENTON HISTORICAL SOCIETY, 1908

Workers and sons gathered in front of the High Point Hotel.

the 1860s and 1870s were Civil War veterans who took advantage of government land grants.

Others were immigrants from Western Europe, such as Austrian cabinetmaker John Zwiefelhofer, who built a cabin in 1879 in what would become Bellevue, and German-born baker William Meydenbauer, who homesteaded land along the bay that now bears his name.

Scandinavians were the first settlers to arrive in larger numbers. Many were loggers who came from tree-clad northern Sweden — some of them directly from the old country, others from Michigan and the upper Midwest — attracted by the tall old-growth forests of the Eastside.

Like many immigrant groups, they sought the company of their kind. Neighborhoods appeared and soon gained monikers that persist, such as Little and Big Finn Hill and Swede Hill, in the Juanita area.

The Preston area east of modern-day Issaquah was called "Little Sweden." One mill owner, John Lovgren, hired only Swedes. Employees were often relatives or immigrants who hailed from the same region back home.

Other Scandinavians were primarily farmers and dairymen. Woodinville's well-known Molbak's nursery is owned by descendants of a Danish family.

"People came to Washington state because they heard about it as the last vestige of prime land," said Marianne Forssblad, executive director of Seattle's Nordic Heritage Museum.

The introduction of the quota system by the U.S. government in the early 1920s stemmed the huge influx of Scandinavian immigrants, said Forssblad.

By the early 1880s, the construction of local railroads able to cart coal to market meant miners were needed in coal-rich spots around Issaquah and Newcastle. Immigrants — Irish, Italian, Welsh, German, Scottish, Belgian, Croatian and Slovakian — all answered the call of the "Pennsylvania of the West."

An aged warning sign for miners, now in a Black Diamond museum, urges caution in more than a dozen languages.

The first notable influx of African Americans arrived from Iowa, Missouri and Illinois in 1891 to work in the Newscastle coal mines. Many of them left within a decade to chase Yukon gold or to farm the Yakima Valley, according to a history by Esther Hall Mumford called "Calabash."

Mining continued into the middle of the century in some places, and those who originally formed ethnic

The track-maintenance crew at the mines in Newcastle reflects the range of immigrants who came seeking work.

An African-American congregation poses in front of its Kennydale church in the 1890s.

enclaves eventually merged into a larger Eastside community.

How well did these groups get along? Fairly well, say local historians. Indians worked alongside immigrants in Issaquah's hops fields.

One documented black settler made his home near Totem Lake near the turn of the century, and history records "no problems at all," according to Alan Stein, president of the Association of King County Historical Organizations.

The notable exception was what came to be known as "the Chinese problem." In 1885, 37 Chinese were brought to modern-day Issaquah by a Chinese firm and the hop-growing Wold Brothers company.

The Chinese spurred resentment among local hops pickers because they were willing to work for lower wages. On Sept. 7, a group of whites and Snoqualmie Indians fired into Chinese tents, killing three and wounding three. No one went to prison.

The incident was part of a larger xenophobia around the area and the West. That year, masked white men also set fire to the building where Chinese workers lived near the Coal Creek mine.

After Seattle mobs put 400 Chinese on outbound trains, President Grover Cleveland in 1886 had to declare martial law in the city.

In 1924, at least 13,000 people attended a Ku Klux

Klan rally in Issaquah.

"I know in the '30s there were groups of black families who tried to move to Juanita, and they encountered some resistance," Stein said. "It wasn't so much their race as the number of them."

No one felt the highs and lows of Eastside life like the Japanese, who planted strawberries and other crops in the shade of old stumps left by logging.

By the 1920s and 1930s, the Japanese were the largest nonwhite ethnic group on the Eastside, their

Above, in the 1990s Hispanic populations increased, along with a demand for ethnic foods.

These Chinese workers were sketched at a coal mine in Renton.

A Laotian immigrant prepares for the Lao Fire Rocket Festival.

ALAN BERNER / THE SEATTLE TIMES, 1998

Bellevue's Japanese population built a community center in 1930 near Northeast 10th Street and 102nd Avenue.

the shipyard in Kirkland, which employed some 6,000 people during the war years.

After the war, the stew of groups that had arrived — from "Okies" to blacks — sometimes chose to put down roots. That didn't sit so well with all members of the community. A front-page story in the Eastside Journal in 1946 was headlined, "Racial Problems Topic of Meeting."

Overall, however, Eastside high-school yearbooks over the next 25 years show "a sea of white faces," said Stein.

That began to change after the Vietnam War. The bloodshed in Southeast Asia brought Vietnamese, Laotian and Cambodian refugees to the area in the 1980s.

Some of the state's 1,200 Hmong, a Laotian hill people, settled and still farm in Carnation. Starting in the late 1980s, people leaving a crumbling Soviet Union began to arrive, especially from Ukraine.

The Hispanic population in almost every city in King County doubled between 1990 and 2000. In Bellevue, it grew to nearly 6,000 people, many of them arriving from California in search of work.

Today the level of diversity varies widely across Eastside cities. U.S. census figures show Bellevue's population was more than 17 percent Asian in 2000, for example, whereas in Duvall and Snoqualmie, Asians comprised just 2 percent of the population. Overall, about one in four Bellevue residents in 2000 was born outside the United States.

Some of that influx can be attributed to the rise of the Eastside's high-tech economy in the 1990s. Redmond, the home of Microsoft, had an Asian Indian population of 3 percent in 2000 — a small number, but growing.

Steve Cohn, an economic planner for Bellevue who has tracked population changes, said the trend toward greater ethnic diversity is likely to continue.

"Diversity is clearly moving out to the suburbs," he said.

faces prominent in school pictures of the time. Japanese produce farms flourished in what's now Bellevue.

That all changed in 1942. With the start of World War II, 443 Japanese Americans from the Eastside were sent to internment camps, including more than 300 from Bellevue. The internees were one-quarter of Bellevue's population. After the war, most didn't return.

The war effort did bring in a surge of other residents, however. People who had fled the Dust Bowl and Depression by working on the Grand Coulee Dam and other projects moved to the Eastside to work at

Sources include: Lucile McDonald's "Bellevue: Its First 100 Years" and Lucile and Richard K. McDonald's "The Coals of Newcastle" and Esther Hall Mumford's "Calabash: A Guide to the History, Culture and Art of African Americans in Seattle and King County, Washington."

Immigration timeline:

Pre-1855: As many as 4,000 Snoqualmies lived in encampments and villages throughout the Eastside, while Duwamish tribal members lived near the south end of Lake Washington.

1860s and 1870s: A mix of Seattleites, European immigrants and Civil War veterans taking advantage of land grants occupy the Eastside.

1880s: Scandinavians begin to arrive, drawn often by logging. Over the next 30 to 40 years, their presence is the largest of any group of immigrants on the Eastside

Late 1880s and 1890s: The coal mines of Newcastle and present-day Issaquah bring an influx of immigrants— Irish, Italian, Welsh, German, Scottish, Belgian, Croatian and Slovakian. African Americans come, too, mostly from the Midwest.

1920s: Japanese farmers establish truck farms, many in the greater Bellevue area.

1942: Most Japanese farmers are sent to internment camps and do not return; the war effort brings thousands of Americans of different backgrounds to work at Boeing and Eastside shipyards in Kirkland and Bellevue.

Late 1970s and 1980s: Turmoil in Southeast Asia brings Vietnamese, Cambodians and Laotians.

Late 1980s: Refugees from the crumbling Soviet Union, especially Ukrainians, begin to arrive.

1990s: Hispanic populations surge in Eastside cities.

Mid-1990s to present: The high-tech industry begins to attract Asian Indians and other Asians.

A Russian immigrant helps out at the food bank in Bellevue.

GREG GILBERT / THE SEATTLE TIMES, 2002

In the late 1980s refugees from Bosnia began arriving on the Eastside.

THOMAS HURST / THE SEATTLE TIMES, 2000

The wives of Microsoft workers from India gather to talk about life in the U.S.

JIM BATES / THE SEATTLE TIMES, 2002

CHAPTER 13

THE RAILROADS

Freeways of commerce from the 1880s to the late 1940s

MARYMOOR MUSEUM OF EASTSIDE HISTORY

Railroads opened the Eastside more than 100 years ago.

They carried coal out of mines in Issaquah and the Coal Creek Valley. They carried logs, shingles and lumber from mills stretching from Kirkland to North Bend.

They brought in supplies: the groceries, the hardware, even the workers. When farming replaced mining and logging, the harvest was sent to market on the train.

Like the highways of today, from the 1880s to the late 1940s, railroads were the lifeblood of civilization, the freeways of commerce. Settlements barely existed without rail connections.

Roads were muddy, stump-filled trails. A trip from Seattle to Ellensburg took four to eight days by horse or foot. After the Milwaukee Road went through Snoqualmie Pass, it took five hours.

"What people don't know today is everything was hauled here by train," said Henry Dahl, a North Bend resident who was a telegraph operator on the Milwaukee line after World War II. "Groceries, newspapers, hardware, everything."

If people wanted to get anywhere rapidly and conveniently, they went by train. Homemakers would catch a morning train in North Bend to Seattle, shop and return home on an afternoon train.

Dennis Croston of Issaquah tells about growing up during the 1950s and visiting his grandparents on Lake Sammamish, several miles away.

"My cousins and I would hop a train and ride to our grandparents' to swim in the lake," Croston said. "They were freight trains. The crews gave up yelling at us not to do it, and they'd slow down to let us get on and off."

On weekends, when they weren't hauling out coal and timber, the railroads offered Seattle residents excursion trips to Snoqualmie Falls.

When the Milwaukee Road went to Snoqualmie Pass, families used the train for outings. In the summers in the 1930s and '40s they picnicked and picked berries, and in winters ski trains brought skiers to the pass. In 1948, a round-trip train ticket from Seattle cost $1.77.

BY SHERRY GRINDELAND

Spur railroad lines that served sawmills wound through the valleys of the Eastside. This example shows the line going into the Woods and Iverson lumber mill at Hobart about 1913.

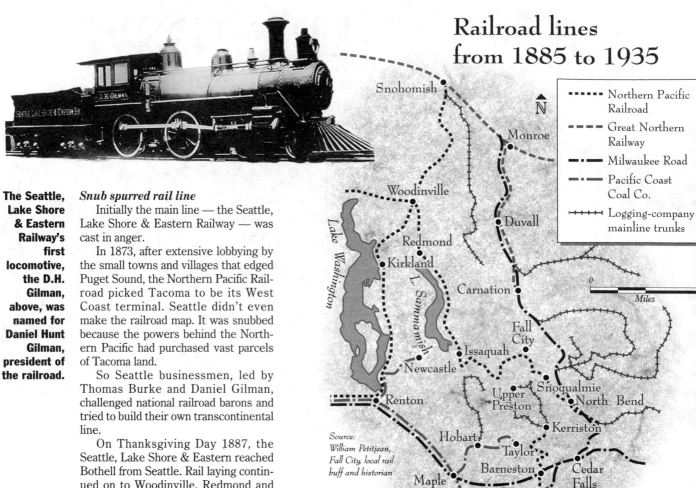

The Seattle, Lake Shore & Eastern Railway's first locomotive, the D.H. Gilman, above, was named for Daniel Hunt Gilman, president of the railroad.

Railroad lines from 1885 to 1935

Northern Pacific Railroad

Great Northern Railway

Milwaukee Road

Pacific Coast Coal Co.

Logging-company mainline trunks

Source: William Petitjean, Fall City local rail buff and historian

THE SEATTLE TIMES

Snub spurred rail line

Initially the main line — the Seattle, Lake Shore & Eastern Railway — was cast in anger.

In 1873, after extensive lobbying by the small towns and villages that edged Puget Sound, the Northern Pacific Railroad picked Tacoma to be its West Coast terminal. Seattle didn't even make the railroad map. It was snubbed because the powers behind the Northern Pacific had purchased vast parcels of Tacoma land.

So Seattle businessmen, led by Thomas Burke and Daniel Gilman, challenged national railroad barons and tried to build their own transcontinental line.

On Thanksgiving Day 1887, the Seattle, Lake Shore & Eastern reached Bothell from Seattle. Rail laying continued on to Woodinville, Redmond and Issaquah, then east to Preston, Snoqualmie and North Bend.

Along the way, founders and investors reaped fortunes, founding mining and lumber companies that worked in the wilderness between Seattle and the Cascades.

In 1896, the Seattle, Lake Shore & Eastern became the Seattle and International Railway, and by 1908 it was part of the Northern Pacific conglomerate.

Today miles of original track have been torn up, but the route of the Seattle, Lake Shore & Eastern is followed by walkers and cyclists along the Burke-Gilman Trail.

It was Gilman who, on a trip back East, convinced Englishman Peter Kirk that the iron deposits in the Cascades and the coal in Newcastle and Issaquah would make this a prime manufacturing area. The Seattle, Lake Shore & Eastern enticed him with a railroad spur. Although Kirk's factory near Forbes Lake never produced an ounce of steel, the city of Kirkland was born with Kirk's investments.

Issaquah, briefly called Gilman, grew up around its depot as coal mining and logging in the area brought in settlers.

First line likely for coal

The first railroad on the Eastside was probably a narrow-gauge line that hauled coal from Coal Creek Valley mines to Lake Washington where it was barged to Seattle.

Around the turn of the century, the Northern Pacific began building the Lake Washington Beltline that would stretch from Renton to Woodinville. Today the Spirit of Washington Dinner Train uses that route.

One persistent legend has it that a train or locomotive fell into a lake and still lies there.

In January 1875, a barge carrying a coal train hit heavy winds and lost its cargo off the north end of Mercer Island.

A salvage operator explored the site in 1994 and says 18 wooden coal cars, many of them still upright and full, sit on the bottom of Lake Washington.

Building railroads in the Eastside hills was difficult, with ravines blocking the way. The easiest solution was giant wooden trestles.

The 984-foot-long Wilburton trestle in Bellevue, built in 1904 just east of Interstate 405, still stands nearly 100 feet above the ground.

Others were taller and longer, including one built near Newcastle in 1877 that stood 138 feet tall and spanned 1,200 feet.

Railroading wasn't only difficult — it was dangerous. Richard Anderson, curator of the Northwest Railway Museum in Snoqualmie, said limbs and lives were lost by crew members. Each car had brakes that had to be individually turned; cars were coupled by hand.

In 1900, a wreck in the Preston-Fall City area killed an engineer, brakeman and fireman when a log fell off a log car and cracked the 100-foot-tall trestle over the Raging River. The engine and numerous cars fell into the riverbed.

Although it was years before the impact rippled into train schedules, the death knell for Eastside lines was struck in the 1920s.

Lake Washington Boulevard was paved for north-south automobile traffic, and in 1928 the Sunset Highway was paved for east-west traffic.

Today less than 40 miles of the original 100-plus miles of Eastside rails remain in use, and railroad buff Bill Walker of North Bend wants to preserve the old stations, rail cars and locomotives that are left. He is documenting the old Upper Snoqualmie Valley lines in a video.

"Historic equipment is like gold," he said. "When these engines and cars and railroad depots are gone, they're gone for good."

This Pacific Coast Coal locomotive was at least 40 years old when this photo was taken along the line that ran through Renton and Maple Valley.

THE SEATTLE TIMES, 1948

TRACKING THE RAILROADS

1867	1873	1887	1890		1904	1909	1942	1989

The first known rail line, a narrow-gauge line built in Coal Creek Valley, transports coal from Newcastle to Lake Washington barges.

The Northern Pacific names Tacoma as the terminus for a transcontinental route; the line reaches Tacoma 10 years later.

The Snoqualmie Depot is built in 60 days. It's now the oldest operating depot in Washington.

The Seattle, Lake Shore & Eastern Railway begins construction; it reaches Bothell on Thanksgiving.

The Milwaukee, St. Paul & Pacific crosses Snoqualmie Pass.

Northern Pacific completes the Lake Washington Beltline, 22 miles connecting Renton, Bellevue, Kirkland and Woodinville.

The Midlakes Station in Bellevue, long used for shipping lettuce, strawberries and other crops, is the departure point for 300 Eastside Japanese Americans sent to internment camps.

Burlington Northern pulls out of the Upper Snoqualmie Valley.

CHAPTER 14

KIRKLAND

Peter Kirk's vision, a steel mill supporting a city of 40,000, was never realized

Peter Kirk

Railroad tracks used to be like the Internet. A century ago, they offered a promise of unparalleled markets and worldwide access.

It was such a promise that made Kirkland.

Trains were reaching never-seen speeds then, and the demand for steel rails seemed limitless, with thousands of miles of tracks needed in the western United States alone.

To Peter Kirk, owner of a steel company in England in 1886, the idea of building a duplicate mill on America's West Coast seemed entirely reasonable.

Exploration showed vast amounts of iron ore in nearby mountains, coal fields to the south, and even needed limestone at quarries on San Juan Island.

Everything seemed poised for Kirk and fellow investors to become the owners of the Microsofts and Compaqs of their age.

Instead, what remains are the oldest buildings on the Eastside and a reminder of how dreams don't always come true.

Settling on Yarrow Bay

Kirkland actually started along what's now called Yarrow Bay.

In the summer of 1872, Harry French, who'd come from Maine with his family, sailed a rented boat from Seattle to the Yarrow Bay shore. He built a cabin of shakes and logs across from where the Bay Shore Apartments now stand on Lake Washington Boulevard.

By 1874, he'd built a wood-frame house, the first in the community. (The house still stands today, moved a bit south to 4130 Lake Washington Blvd. N.E.)

Other settlers followed, including the Curtis family, who arrived from South Dakota and built near the Frenches. The family began operating freight and ferry boats and by 1901 was building boats as well, creating a business that would later play a key role in Kirkland history.

As the settlement grew, a church was needed and a

This photo of Kirkland was taken about 1907 from the hill east of Market Street between Second and Third streets. The view was south toward Lake Street, now part of Lake Washington Boulevard.

BY PEYTON WHITELY

KIRKLAND IRON WORKS KIRKLAND, WASH.

OLD SEATTLE PAPERWORKS

Daniel Gilman

church needed a bell, which was produced by a New York foundry for $184.50.

The cost was paid by Sarah J. Houghton, wife of a Boston philanthropist who became interested in the Kirkland congregation through a church in Providence, R.I.

The settlement, which had been using the name Pleasant Bay, was renamed Houghton in their honor.

The bell survives, standing atop the south end of the Kirkland Congregational church at First Street and Fifth Avenue.

For most of those early years, until the late 1880s, what's now downtown Kirkland was just two marshy homesteads owned by John DeMott and Ed Church.

In 1883, however, New York lawyer Daniel Gilman arrived in Seattle and began planning a railroad to connect Seattle to the Issaquah coal fields.

Much of the route of that Seattle, Lake Shore & Eastern Railway remains today as Seattle's Burke-Gilman Trail. Gilman needed rails and got them from Kirk's Moss Bay Hematite Iron & Steel Co. in Workington, England.

The two men first met in New York in 1886 when Kirk, then 46, was interested in expanding his steel business.

By September of that year, he had visited iron deposits in the "Snoqualmie Mountains" and considered placing a mill near North Bend, but he ran into problems trying to purchase property because of his English citizenship.

That's when he met Leigh S. J. Hunt.

Hunt, former president of Iowa State College, moved West about 1884 and purchased a Seattle newspaper named the Post-Intelligencer. He liked the east shore of Lake Washington and named Yarrow Point and Yarrow Bay after two of his favorite Wordsworth poems. He built a house on Yarrow Point in 1886. Hunts Point is named for him.

When Kirk told Hunt of his problems buying land for his mill, Hunt had the solution. By declaring his intent to become a U.S. citizen, Kirk was able to arrange with Hunt to own property through a corporate business structure.

A city of 40,000 envisioned

In July 1888, Hunt, Kirk and other investors formed the Kirkland Land & Improvement Co., buying 1,400 acres in the area now bounded by Central Way, Juanita Slough, Lake Washington and Rose Hill.

A few months later, the Moss Bay Iron & Steel Works of America was incorporated. In 1890 it was reorganized as the Great Western Iron & Steel Works of America.

A city of 40,000 was visualized.

At first, plans were to build the steel mill at what's now Peter Kirk Park.

But when Kirk learned the railroad would come south from Woodinville only as far as Rose Hill, he moved the mill site just north of today's Costco, along Forbes Lake. By March 1891, a sawmill on the lake had cut 3 million board feet of lumber, pits had been dug for blast furnaces and a foundry and a 160-by-34-foot cast house had been built.

The center of town was to be what's now Seventh Avenue and Market Street, where the Eastside's oldest commercial buildings still stand.

Within a few months, the plans collapsed.

The Tacoma Ledger newspaper printed an "exposé" declaring the steel plans were a ploy by Hunt

In 1888 Leigh S.J. Hunt, Peter Kirk and other investors bought land in the area now bounded by Central Way, Juanita Slough, Lake Washington and Rose Hill. A few months later, the Moss Bay Iron & Steel Works of America, above, was incorporated.

Leigh Hunt

This group of brick build- ings, near what's now Market Street and Seventh were sup- posed to be the center of the steel city.

THE SEATTLE TIMES, 1948

and other investors to get rich on land deals.

The Northern Pacific didn't finish the tracks to the iron mines east of North Bend.

And an English bank failure led to hundreds of American bank failures, the Panic of 1893, and East Coast investors' inability to keep putting money into Kirkland.

The steel plant was abandoned in December 1893 before it even opened.

Kirk remained solvent and later formed the Kirk- land Development Co., but in 1910, saddened by the death of a daughter, he sold the company to two Seat- tle businessmen, Edmund Burke and Bert Farrar. For decades they ran real-estate offices at the Kirkland and Seattle ferry landings, selling Kirkland city lots for $75. Kirk moved to San Juan Island and died there in 1916.

Hunt lost nearly everything in the mill failure and sold the P-I. He went on to a life that might make a good novel, however: gold mining in North Korea, becoming wealthy enough to repay his Seattle credi- tors, developing cotton plantations in the Sudan and finally getting interested in the building of Hoover Dam and moving to Las Vegas, where he died in 1933.

Kirkland became known as "stump city" because of the desolation left from the 1890s land clearing.

The potential of the waterfront

It was shipbuilding that eventually brought some prosperity to the town. The Lake Washington Ship- yards developed on what had been the Curtis home- stead and employed more than 6,000 workers during World War II. Ferry traffic also grew, and for many years Kirkland was the largest city on the Eastside.

The completion of the first Lake Washington Float- ing Bridge in 1940 led to Bellevue's eventual rise as the biggest Eastside city. For the next 40 years, Kirkland struggled as new suburban shopping centers — includ- ing Bellevue Square — stole much of its business.

The Evergreen Point Floating Bridge brought new access in 1963, and community leaders recognized the potential of the city's waterfront, acquiring thousands of feet of public shoreline.

An active historical organization, the Kirkland Her- itage Society, now fights to preserve the city's past, putting up descriptive markers and seeking to make history a part of community-character guidelines.

By the early 1970s, Kirkland had begun changing to the beach-restaurant-gallery place it has become today, with much of its prosperity attributed to high- tech businesses in the surrounding area.

One part of Peter Kirk's vision did come true: In 1998 Kirkland's estimated population was 43,160. Kirk's prediction was off by only a century.

Sources include "Our Foundering Fathers, The Story of Kirkland," by Arline Ely, Kirkland Public Library, 1975;
"The Lake Washington Story," by Lucile McDonald, Superior Publishing Co., Seattle, 1979;
"History of Kirkland," an unindexed collection of various newspaper articles maintained by the King County Library System;
"Washington, West of the Cascades," by Herbert Hunt and Floyd C. Kaylor, published by S.J. Clarke Publishing Co., 1917;
and "History of Seattle, Washington," edited by Frederic James Grant, American Publishing and Engraving Co., 1891.

CHAPTER 15

REDMOND

The McRedmond family prevailed in a decades-long feud over the town's name

MARYMOOR MUSEUM OF EASTSIDE HISTORY

If not for the wily clan McRedmond, the software town known round the world might be Melrose.

Redmond was renamed several times after the first white families arrived in 1871, causing squabbles among the pioneers and hard feelings that remain today among their descendants.

Luke McRedmond **Warren Perrigo**

This photo of downtown Redmond, looking west on Cleveland Street, was taken in 1912, the year the city incorporated.

Luke McRedmond was there first — but only by a whisker, and the Irish adventurer didn't bother with the name until years later.

Melrose was the name given to the town in the 1870s by the second family to arrive, a young couple recruited from Maine by Seattle booster Asa Mercer.

William and Laura Perrigo soon built a hotel for the pioneers, hunters and travelers crossing Snoqualmie Pass.

They named it Melrose House after a beloved town near Boston.

The hotel, near what's now Value Village on Redmond Way, became a focal point for the scattered homesteads that formed the early community.

Soon everyone started calling the place Melrose, including U.S. postal authorities, who opened a Melrose post office in 1881.

Melrose eased the homesickness of the transplanted New Englanders, and it sounded better than Salmonberg. That's what the area was called earlier because of its fish-clogged streams.

As the hotel prospered, Warren Perrigo was

BY BRIER DUDLEY

William Perrigo (white beard in back center), poses with family members and others at the Perrigo Trading Post in 1902.

joined by his younger brother, William, who started a trading post that grew to serve the whole Sammamish Valley.

William Perrigo also became active in real estate and regional politics, joining a coalition of businessmen advocating for roads to link cities in the Puget Sound area.

Later he donated land for the city's first water system, a Methodist church, a cemetery and the historic Redmond Elementary School that's now a community center.

Melrose wasn't sitting well with Luke McRedmond, however.

Dangerous times

It was a wonderland of towering forests, misty marshes and curious Native Americans when McRedmond's family of seven arrived in the spring of 1871, settling on the river plain that's now the Redmond Town Center shopping center and business park.

They had sold a house at First and Madison in downtown Seattle, loaded their possessions onto a scow and rowed for days up the 60-mile maze of streams from Puget Sound.

Like suburbanites a century later, they had left the bustling city in search of more land and a new beginning.

But unlike today's urban refugees drawn by the notion of safety in the suburbs, the McRedmonds and Perrigos were venturing into potentially dangerous territory.

The first settlers in Issaquah had been killed by Native Americans seven years earlier, and it hadn't been long since Seattle was ransacked during the Indian War of 1855.

But the uncharted wilds of the Eastside were there for the taking under the Homestead Act, which offered tracts to anyone who paid a $10 fee, improved the land and stayed for at least five years.

These pioneer families were no strangers to adventure. McRedmond left Ireland during the potato famine of 1850, traveled across the United States to the Cali-

fornia gold rush and served as Kitsap County sheriff before homesteading.

Warren Perrigo, grandson of a French Corsican soldier who fought for America in the Revolutionary War, was a Civil War hero who left the front after suffering from yellow fever.

He found little farmland available at home in Maine, so he and Laura boarded a ship full of young women Mercer had recruited as brides for pioneer men and sailed around Cape Horn to Seattle.

Teaching school in Kitsap County and working at a Seattle sawmill didn't quench Perrigo's wanderlust, so he and Laura filed their claim for 80 acres in June 1871.

By 1880, when the Kirkland-Redmond Road opened up the first wagon route to the outside world, there were 50 families who had slowly cleared homes and farms from the forest.

They used hot coals to burn the base off the giant cedars until they fell, then hauled the logs around with oxen teams.

No community would be complete without intrigues, and soon the McRedmonds and their friends began maneuvering to change the name from Melrose.

William Perrigo gave land for Redmond Elementary School, seen here around 1922.

William Perrigo's daughter Mabel Johnson, left, and another cyclist in 1904.

MARYMOOR MUSEUM OF EASTSIDE HISTORY

In December 1882 McRedmond was appointed postmaster and quickly petitioned postal authorities to change the office's name to Redmond.

In March 1883 his request was granted, but the Perrigos were stubborn.

Perrigo relatives on the East Coast continued addressing mail to Melrose for years.

After McRedmond's daughter Emma became postmistress in 1885, she was said to have crossed Melrose off the letters and written in Redmond.

The final blow came when McRedmond donated land for a new Redmond railway station, and soon Melrose faded from memory.

Meanwhile, Laura Perrigo fell ill and died in 1887, and Warren gave up the hotel and moved back to Seattle in 1892.

William and his wife, Matilda, stayed and prospered, raising a family of 11 and eventually acquiring 777 acres between Avondale Way and Redmond-Woodinville Road.

Their 1909 home on Avondale Road is a historic landmark though it's now encircled by a condominium complex.

Pioneer ghosts linger

The city was incorporated as Redmond in 1912 with a population of 300. Today it's home to 43,610 people and the world's largest software company, which has made Redmond synonymous in computer circles with Microsoft.

Although the Perrigos lost the name battle, the family has grown to over 500 members, many of whom remain in the area. A few McRedmond descendants live locally.

But the ghost of old Luke McRedmond may be lingering around the city to foil the Perrigos' quest for recognition.

Since the early 1980s the Perrigos have been asking the city to name something after the family.

In 1998 the Parks Board rejected a proposal by Wendy Conover of Kirkland — William Perrigo's great-granddaughter — to name the old schoolhouse after him. Instead the board recommended naming the building "The Old Redmond Schoolhouse Community Center."

The board said it was reserving the Perrigo name for a future use, perhaps for a park.

Sources include Wendy Conover, "Our Town Redmond" by Nancy Way, and "Squak Slough 1870-1920" by Eunice Stickney and Lucile McDonald.

CHAPTER 16

POWER TO THE PEOPLE

The plant Charles Baker started building in 1898 still powers 16,000 homes

While the 1.5 million visitors who stop at Snoqualmie Falls each year marvel at the waterfall that is nearly 100 feet higher than Niagara Falls, few know that the south side of the cliff contains the world's first underground hydro-electric plant. Or that the 100-year-old equipment still turns out enough power to light 16,000 homes.

Charles Baker, the man who built the plant, dreamed bigger. He bragged it would provide electricity for every town from Bellingham to Olympia. He was a better builder than businessman or visionary.

A century ago electric lights were considered an on-again, off-again thing. Mill towns such as Bothell often had them, a fringe benefit from the steam generators that operated the heavy equipment. The mining town of Newcastle was also company-powered.

Seattle wasn't. But competitive entrepreneurs had bright hopes.

Baker began construction of the Snoqualmie plant in April 1898.

On July 31, 1899, his 18-month-old daughter, Dorothy, threw the switch that put the plant online. Electricity went from Snoqualmie Falls to a substation in Issaquah, then on to Renton where it was dispersed to Seattle and Tacoma.

It was the first long-distance transmission facility in the Northwest.

Father-son team succeeds

The Cornell University-educated Baker came to the Northwest to do engineering work for the Seattle Lake Shore & Eastern Railroad. He helped design the rail lines that reached Snoqualmie Falls in 1889.

An early photograph shows Baker fishing in the river below the falls.

He left the railroad and contracted with Seattle pioneer David Denny to build the Third Street and Suburban Electric Railway.

Both Baker and Denny were caught in the financial crisis of 1893, losing their investments. Baker ended

Charles Baker

A man believed to be Charles Baker fishes at the base of the falls around 1890 — before the power plant, observation decks and tourist facilities were built.

PUGET SOUND ENERG

BY SHERRY GRINDELAND

up $60,000 in debt, a huge sum at the time.

Baker then worked on several deals, trying to buy options on all the streetcar lines in Seattle, the land around Snoqualmie Falls and also build the power plant.

Without a bankroll, Baker took his proposal to his father, William T. Baker.

The elder Baker was both wealthy and well-connected; he was president of the Chicago Board of Trade and had organized the highly successful World's Columbian Exposition, the 1893 world's fair in Chicago.

To keep the younger Baker's creditors at bay, everything was put in the elder Baker's name, even though the two considered themselves partners. Nothing about the partnership was put in writing, a mistake the younger Baker regretted after his father's death in October 1903.

A remarkable building feat

Baker built the power plant underground to protect the machinery from the constant mist of the falls and from winter's freezing weather. One photograph taken during the construction shows the entire cliff, falls and construction site enveloped in ice.

Laborers worked around the clock, drilling and dynamiting a shaft that went 270 feet from the top of the falls to the riverbed.

A huge cave was created at the bottom of the shaft, 200 feet by 40 feet by 30 feet, to contain four turbines. Bore holes remain visible today in the rock cavity. Much of the cavity was whitewashed, making it look eerily bright despite being 270 feet below ground.

River water flows down the shaft through pipes — called penstocks — to the turbines. It is then released into a 450-foot-long tailrace — or stream bed carved out of the basalt. A narrow wooden walk, suspended on

The Snoqualmie Falls Hotel, pictured here about 1893, was on the south side of the falls, across from the present-day Salish Lodge.

PUGET SOUND ENERGY

MORE THAN A CENTURY OF TOURISM

Snoqualmie Falls was a popular tourist attraction well before the power station was built.

The site was sacred to members of the Snoqualmie and Yakama nations, who met near the falls for trading and winter camping.

The first white man to see the falls was probably a surveyor, Washington Hall.

After the railroads came in 1889, a depot was built just above the falls on the south side of the river, quickly followed by the first Snoqualmie Falls Hotel. Built between the railroad and the falls, the hotel featured an open-air dance floor built out over the chasm.

The Snoqualmie Falls Lodge was built in 1919 across the river from the plant, separating tourists

from the transformers and high voltage wires. A footbridge for plant workers was added in 1932.

The lodge has undergone several transformations, becoming today's Salish Lodge in 1987.

A 1949 earthquake caused a wall of rock near the lodge to crack and tumble into the gorge. The latest covered observation deck was added in 1968.

Inside the power plant much remains from Baker's day. The seven-eighths-inch thick steel pipes bringing the water to the turbines are the same ones he installed. A lighted display panel with the date, 1898, still hangs at the end of the cavity.

The catwalk still goes out to the base of the falls, resting on steel beams just like it did in 1899.

steel beams, follows the tailrace to the river at the bottom of the falls.

Set back from the top of the falls is a submerged concrete dam to control the flow of the river. At the lip of the falls, a giant boulder called Seattle Rock was partly blasted away.

Not one workman was killed or injured in the project, remarkable considering the dismal safety record of railroads and lumber mills.

Today a modern elevator transports visitors from the top to bottom in a two-minute ride. The first elevator was water-powered; if the operator wasn't paying enough attention to apply the hand brake, it would bounce at the bottom and make the round trip back up to the top without stopping.

Competition and smear

By the time the plant was built, Baker's main competitors were Charles Stone and Edwin Webster, who had several generating stations in Seattle. The two had gained control of all the streetcar lines that would eventually become the Interurban rail system. Baker planned another power plant near Tacoma.

A smear campaign said Baker's power was unreliable because it was so far away. Soon after, in 1903, a fire destroyed the elevator, transformer building and all but one generator. Snoqualmie Falls Power Plant was out of operation for 36 hours and limited service for another three weeks. Baker later wrote that he believed the fire was arson.

A fifth generator was added to the plant in 1905. Ironically the newest piece of equipment is the one that doesn't work today. It sits, partly torn apart, still in place.

In 1910 a second power station, on the north side and downstream from the falls, was added. The penstocks for that system go under the rock cliff that today is the base for the Salish Lodge.

Baker didn't have anything to do with the second plant. After his father's death, the estate lawyers refused to consider Charles Baker a partner and by 1908 had sold Snoqualmie Falls Power and the Seattle Cataract and Tacoma Cataract companies to Seattle-Tacoma Power, forerunner of today's Puget Sound Energy conglomerate.

The purchasers were Stone and Webster, Baker's main competitors.

PUGET SOUND ENERGY

Construction of the original power plant involved digging a shaft 270 feet from the top of the falls to the riverbed. Workers moved tons of basalt but there were no serious injuries, despite working in freezing weather that froze the falls and turned the face of the cliff into an ice palace.

CHAPTER 17

LIQUOR AND LUST

This was the frontier, with plenty of rowdy men and illicit enterprises

SNOQUALMIE VALLEY HISTORICAL MUSEUM

A dance hall predated any church buildings within Issaquah city limits. Even when organized religion arrived, taverns outnumbered houses of worship.

So did men. Until the 1920s, males outnumbered females 2-1 in the Northwest. And on the Eastside, most of those men were young, strong miners, loggers, millworkers and farmers with appetites for booze, brawls, card games and evenings with wanton women.

In the Eastside's earliest days, when lumber mills and mining towns were company-run affairs, workers would go to Seattle for liquor and female companionship. But as the small towns boomed, hotels blossomed to accommodate both the housing and recreational needs of transient lumber and mining crews.

One entertaining aspect was drinking.

Loggers, miners and railroad men liked their liquid refreshment. In 1907, when the Milwaukee Railroad was being built, King County granted 31 saloon licenses for the North Bend area alone. Tavern owners set up card rooms for a cut of the action.

Parties got rowdy.

"There's a reason the old Issaquah jail, used from 1914 to 1924, was made of cement," said Nancy Horrocks of the Issaquah Historical Society. "Wood wouldn't hold the miners or loggers. They were so tough they would kick their way out of a wooden cell."

Defying Prohibition

When the 18th Amendment to the U.S. Constitution banned liquor — from 1919 to 1933 — the East-

Local taverns could be rowdy places in the early part of the century. Here patrons at the U&I Bar in North Bend pose for a calendar photo around 1910.

BY SHERRY GRINDELAND

Taverns outnumbered churches in the early days of Eastside towns and were gathering places for miners, loggers and millworkers. This photo was taken in the Hotel Bellevue bar in downtown Issaquah before 1914.

ISSAQUAH HISTORICAL SOCIETY

side was anything but dry. Old-timers joke about the "night lights" — fires from whiskey stills hidden in the woods and valleys could be seen from any hilltop.

David Horrocks cautions against judging local hooch entrepreneurs harshly because Prohibition was so unpopular. His family property south of the city was rented out during that era. When family members moved back, they discovered alterations. Wainscoting in the dining room concealed a storage area with moonshine.

Horrocks literally stumbled into a still, falling through a hole in the back yard that was an underground room containing copper tubing, tanks, shelves and bottles.

"We had bottles of the moonshine in the fruit room for a long time," said his wife Nancy. "Stills were known to be all over the place."

It was easy to get the ingredients. Any farmer with chickens could order extra corn mash. Sugar was sold for cash and, according to another late historian Edwards Fish, was shipped to the Eastside by the carload.

Making it was one thing; selling it was another.

One known outlet was The Blind Pig by Lake Washington in the Juanita area, says Kirkland historian Alan Stein. Evidence could be poured into the lake when a raid was pending.

The late historian Lucile McDonald, who interviewed many early settlers, identified the location of several stills, including one on Market Street in downtown Kirkland, one in Juanita, and one near the intersection of 23rd Street Southeast and 108th Avenue in Bellevue.

Neighbors near the latter got suspicious when the laundry hung out to dry consisted only of whiskey-stained tea towels, but by the time officials were alerted, the renters had disappeared.

A local taxi operator was known to deliver whiskey as well as passengers, according to historian Nancy Way in her book, "Our Town Redmond."

The Stone House in downtown Redmond has also been cited as a Prohibition-era drinking establishment, as well as several former resorts on both Lake Washington and Lake Sammamish. Many were billed as dance halls. (During Prohibition, dance halls were pop-

ular legitimate entertainment centers patronized by all economic classes.)

Brothels a booming business

Although rumors and folklore abound about hotels that were fronts for brothels, corroborative materials are rare. Such establishments rarely rate bronze memorial plaques from early historians, usually womenfolk who ignored such human frailties.

A former hotel and house in Snoqualmie have been identified as brothels by Richard Anderson, curator at the Northwest Railway Museum in Snoqualmie and Upper Snoqualmie Valley historian David Battey.

The Blind Pig, mentioned as a liquor outlet, also supposedly offered friendly females.

A bartender waits to serve in Clark's Place in downtown Issaquah sometime before 1910. Over the years there were several establishments run by the Clark family, including a popular pool hall.

ISSAQUAH HISTORICAL SOCIETY

In this photo from the 1890s, a pack train stops outside the North Bend Gustin & Tibbets' Cascadia Hotel. As the Eastside's small towns boomed, hotels often served both the housing and recreational needs of the largely male population.

According to two longtime Bellevue residents, one mainstream establishment ran a legitimate business by day while at night male customers used the alley door for entrance to a small brothel.

Flesh shows have had people up in arms as recently as 1995 when Bellevue citizens fought the topless dance club Papagayo's in the Fred Meyer Shopping Center.

There have been others.

Woodinville's Good Time Charlie's, a topless dance club, closed in 1985. Bavarian Gardens in Factoria, which closed in the early 1980s, featured a 400-pound dancer named Big Fannie Annie. Babe's, a male strip club, operated briefly in Factoria in 1995.

Redmond once had an X-rated movie theater.

A Bothell soda-pop bar called Mama Hoopah's opened in 1982 and law- enforcement officials made many arrests for prostitution, lewd conduct, sale and possession of drugs and selling alcohol without a liquor license.

The owners had neglected to get an adult-dance-club permit so Bothell closed it six months later.

A few of the early taverns still exist as community watering holes.

Issaquah resident Walt Seil, whose grandparents homesteaded on Tiger Mountain tells a family story about one tavern, now called the Rollin Log, on East Sunset Way in downtown Issaquah.

The city was still small — fewer than 1,000 residents — in the 1940s when Seil's father, Ed "Nogs" Seil served as town marshall.

"Dad kept the peace without lawyers and judges," Seil said.

One night Nogs was called to handle an uproar in a local tavern. The ruckus began when a 90-year-old gentleman bought an 80-year-old woman a beer. The 90-year-old verbally and physically objected when another man tried to buy the woman a drink.

Nogs led the 90-year-old to jail but left the cell door unlocked. From the shadows across the street, Nogs and Seil watched as the 90-year-old peered out of city hall. He then scurried down the street to his nearby home.

"The 90-year-old was my grandfather," Seil said.

CHAPTER 18

THE WILD, WILD EAST

Shoot-'em-up robberies were big news locally during the Roaring '20s

THE SEATTLE TIMES, 1925

Gunfire shattered the quiet downtown area of Bothell as three masked men in a stolen car escaped in a hail of bullets with about $3,000 in loot from the Bothell State Bank. The bank president gave chase but was left in the dust near Kirkland.

When it was over, two members of the River Rat Gang from Everett were dead and two others were arrested.

It was June 5, 1925, the middle of the Roaring '20s.

Rogers Hornsby and Harry Heilmann were on their way to winning batting championships in the National and American leagues.

The Washington Huskies and Navy had played to a 14-14 draw in the Rose Bowl, while varsity rowers placed second and junior varsity took top honors in the National Intercollegiate Rowing Regatta in Poughkeepsie, N.Y.

Bothell was a thriving community of about 600, mostly loggers, sawmill and shingle-mill workers, produce and dairy farmers and people who worked in local businesses.

A "Wild West" atmosphere lingered those days on the Eastside, which was far removed from the more urban Seattle area across Lake Washington.

Shootings, stabbings, drunken brawls and free-for-all fights were common in the small logging and mining towns scattered along the lake and in the close-in Cascade foothills from Black Diamond to Duvall.

Bank robberies, though, were big news, and two shoot-'em-up-style heists in Bothell and Carnation caught the public's attention.

Articles from The Seattle Daily Times describe that June day in Bothell when carpenter Thomas Underhill first saw the black Buick touring car with the

An arrow marks the Bothell State Bank, on Bothell's Main Street, where a shootout and robbery occurred in June 1925.

BY LOUIS T. CORSALETTI

THE SEATTLE TIMES, 1924

Members of the King County Sheriff's department who foiled the Snoqualmie Valley Bank robbery pose with Jack E. Bench, who drove the bandits' automobile. From left: Deputy Sheriff C.H. Beebe, Deputy Frank Anderson, Bench, Deputy Ray E. Murphy, Sheriff Matt Starwich, Deputy Ed Fitzgerald and Deputy Tom Morgan.

three masked men inside drive onto Main Street. Remembering a robbery at the bank the previous January, he shouted a warning and became the first target of the bandits.

One robber leaned from the car and began shooting at Underhill, who dodged behind a parked car that was soon riddled with bullet holes.

The town marshal, S.E. Hitsman, and his son, H.E. Hitsman, ran to a hardware store a few doors from the bank, grabbed rifles and ammunition from behind the counter and climbed to the roof of a pool hall across from the bank.

Entering the bank, one robber held Ross Worley, the bank cashier, and Vaughn Bosley, assistant cashier, at gunpoint while the other rifled cash drawers and grabbed a bag of money from the open safe vault.

The third bandit stood near the front door.

Outside, the driver of the getaway car waited.

As they ran out the bank door, the bandits were greeted by rifle fire from the Hitsmans and later from behind by Worley and Bosley, who had grabbed rifles from the vault.

A shot from Worley's gun hit one robber, who was pulled into the car by his partners. The car sped off as bullets flew.

Bank President A.G. Worthington was outside when the robbers fled, and he jumped into his car, chasing them as far as Kirkland before he was outdistanced.

Two of the robbers were hit by gunfire and died — Jimmy Pollock and George Jones. Another man was wounded and arrested in Portland and the fourth was arrested in Vancouver, Wash.

The loot from the robbery was never recovered.

The bank building still stands on Main Street, now occupied by the Bothell Nutrition store.

Another foiled robbery

Equally spectacular was the foiled bank robbery in Carnation on Thursday, Aug. 13, 1924. It was the stuff dime westerns were made of.

Carnation, incorporated 12 years earlier, was a logging boom town of some 530 residents along the Snoqualmie River.

Tolt Avenue, a wide dirt road, speared through town. Scattered along both sides of the roadway were a variety of businesses, including the Snoqualmie Valley Bank.

The Seattle Daily Times account told this story:

STARWICH AND POSSE FRUSTRATE BOLD GANG

"Dramatically interrupting an attempted daylight hold-up at the Snoqualmie Valley Bank at Carnation, formerly known as Tolt, at 2:15 o'clock yesterday afternoon, Sheriff Matt Starwich and six deputies shot and killed D.C. Malone, alias A.J. Brown, leader of the bandit band, and captured the driver of their automobile."

A few days before, Malone had tried to hold up a Seattle restaurant but couldn't open the cash register. His bad luck continued when he ran up against Starwich, a tough lawman known for his flamboyant style.

On learning of the planned robbery, Starwich staked his deputies around town.

"So confident was Starwich that he invited all newspaper reporters and photographers attached to the Court House to go to Tolt, warning them to remain in hiding until the bandits were caught," reported The Times.

Starwich armed the deputies with sawed-off shotguns and revolvers.

He put three deputies in a small room in the bank while he and two deputies hid in a small shed across the street.

Isadore Hall, bank vice president, agreed to serve as the teller while the regular teller was sent home.

Noon passed; the posse ate lunch and returned to their posts.

At about 2 p.m. a car drove slowly into town, passed the bank, turned around and came back.

Two men jumped out and ran into the bank while one remained at the wheel. Another man approached on foot from where the car had turned around and walked into the bank.

Starwich and his deputies approached the driver.

"Stick 'em up," the sheriff said, according to the story.

"The driver stuttered . . . his hands didn't go up," the story recounts. "Starwich grabbed him by the shoulder, hauled him out of the car and felled him with a blow on his jaw."

Inside the bank, Malone jumped over the counter and then heard Starwich's voice outside. Suddenly, he turned and ran toward the vault only to be met with the bullets of the deputies who stepped from the back room.

Still firing, Malone staggered backward and hit the informant, Ted Lashe, who died later in the day.

Wounded a dozen times, Malone kept firing until he was felled by a shotgun blast and died.

During the exchange, Deputy Virgil Murphy was hit in the left thigh.

Later, deputies figured more than 50 shots were fired during the melee.

Sources include "A History of Tolt/Carnation, A Town Remembered" by Isabel L. Jones.

MATT STARWICH WAS THE LAW

King County Sheriff Matt Starwich was a legend in his own time, often using his fists instead of a gun to take a criminal into custody.

The short, strong, barrel-chested Austrian immigrant who spoke six languages was pressed into a sheriff's posse in 1902 tracking down the notorious "Cayuse Harry" Tracy who once headed up the famed Hole In The Wall Gang.

Tracy showed up in the Seattle area on the lam, killing a sheriff's deputy in a Bothell shootout and later a Seattle police officer before heading out to cross the Cascades on foot. He was finally cornered in a hayfield in Creston, Lincoln County. Hit by gunfire, he shot himself in the head.

Starwich's role in the hunt won the respect of the county commissioners, who appointed him deputy sheriff of the small coal-mining town of Ravensdale east of Kent.

Miners soon came to respect him. One story tells about the time five laborers got roaring drunk, terror-

Matt Starwich

ized the village and took over the railroad station. The flamboyant Starwich walked into the station, methodically knocked the five men out, cuffed them and hauled them to jail.

Another time a man shot and killed two Ravensdale brothers and then holed up in a vacant building. Starwich is said to have kicked the door down and, after dodging three shots from the man's pistol, knocked him out and dragged him outside.

And there was the riot in which Starwich arrested so many men he had to commandeer a coach on a passing passenger train to haul the prisoners to the county jail in Seattle.

Starwich was finally elected sheriff in 1920 and held office until his retirement in 1926.

Eight years later, he lost the sheriff's race to William Severyns, who turned around and appointed him county jail superintendent, a post he held until his death on Dec. 6, 1941.

CHAPTER 19

DUVALL

Its early move to make way for the railroad created a transplant with deep roots

DUVALL HISTORICAL SOCIETY

When Arthur and Pauline Hix arrived in the Snoqualmie River Valley from Indiana in 1905 to build a little house and a general store, they found a fledgling village ready to become a town.

Already a Methodist church, a saloon and a tiny schoolhouse hugged the hillside above the waterway, serving the loggers working the surrounding foothills and the sparse population of homesteaders sowing their livings into the fertile valley soil.

Decades earlier, the first postmaster, Lucius Day, had been asked to name the hamlet. Legend has it he looked out the window onto an orchard, blooming snowy pink in a springtime meadow. And he declared, "Let's call it Cherry Valley."

But it wasn't to be. The railroad was coming. And Cherry Valley was right in the way.

So in winter 1909, the Hixes and the other townsfolk did the logical thing for the time: They picked up their buildings, loaded them on logging skids and braces, and for the next two months hauled them, intact, a half a mile south to a different history — a town called Duvall.

"Arthur Hix, Cherry Valley's pioneer merchant, has commenced moving his store farther south," the Monroe Monitor reported at the time. "The line of the railroad runs through the old store — in one side and out the other — but even with such excellent shipping facilities as would thus be afforded, Mr. Hix desires to move."

Eighty-nine years later, Duvall has grown from scrappy mill town to sleepy farm settlement, passed

Duvall's Main Street in 1910 included, from left, A.P. Manion's hardware store, the Manion Furniture Annex, Brown's confectionery and Moody & Moody, which boasted it had "a $10,000 stock of dry goods, clothing, boots and shoes."

BY IAN IITH

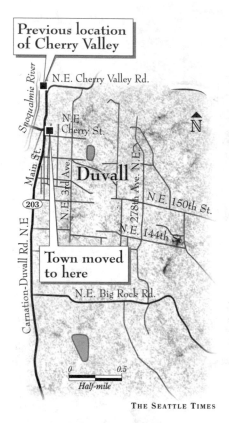

THE SEATTLE TIMES

DUVALL HISTORICAL SOCIET

through a period as something of a haven for hippies and has ended up as a bedroom community for city-fleeing professionals, with subdivisions and businesses popping up like mushrooms.

But the pioneers who still live in the area remain fiercely loyal to the memory of Duvall as it was.

"The streets weren't level or anything, and my father didn't have a customer every day, but when he did it was usually a good one," remembers Velma Hix-Hill, the 85-year-old daughter of Arthur and Pauline Hix who still lives in the home the family hauled up the hill from Cherry Valley in 1910.

She was Duvall's postmaster from 1940 to 1976. Her parents' store still stands as Duvall Auto Parts at Main and Cherry streets.

Built in 1888 by James O'Leary, this was the first home in Cherry Valley. It was moved along with the rest of the town in 1910 and later housed a post office. Pictured here in 1911 are six of the eight children that John and Kate Dougherty raised in the home. It's now being restored as a museum.

Land homesteaded in 1871

James Duvall never actually lived in the city that bears his name.

He left for parts unknown in 1909, a year before the buildings of Cherry Valley were tugged up the hill to join the new ones being built in anticipation of the Great Northern and the Milwaukee railroads plowing through to deliver logs to the many riverside mills.

The city incorporated in 1913.

The land where Duvall sits today was homesteaded in 1871 by James Duvall's brother, Francis. But he sold it several years later, and it eventually ended up in the hands of the Port Blakely Mill.

James Duvall

But in 1887, James Duvall, who had been logging in the Everett area, bought the property and quickly moved his oxen to begin clearing the land. He became famous locally for building tough skids to slide timber into the river. The city streets were later built over them, and, as recently as 1988, some of the grease-coated, wooden slides sometimes poked out of the dirt along the side of Main Street.

In 1890 Duvall's wife, Annie, died soon after their fourth child was born. Looking for quick money to pay off his debts, Duvall set out for Arizona and later to the Yukon in search of gold.

There's no record that he found any. He returned to his land, sold it piece by piece in 1909, and left.

Duvall's departure didn't make a dent in the booming timber economy that would make his namesake thrive. There were trees to be had — big ones. And

Arthur Hix's store is pictured in 1910 after it was hauled uphill from Cherry Valley. Standing in front are E.F. Hanisch, left, and Chris Unger, homesteaders who had land just south of town. Today the building houses Duvall Auto Parts.

The L.T. Smith shingle mill, shown, right, in 1914, employed 40 men at its peak and was one of several on the Snoqualmie River during the logging boom. It operated around the clock and generated electricity for the town.

that meant men, lots of them, to cut them down and saw them up.

The Snoqualmie River was lined with mill after mill as railroads hauled logs out of the hills and dumped them in the water.

Main Street bustled with businesses, including the impressive Forest Inn, a long, three-story hotel and saloon that overlooked the river about where the bridge over the river is today. It burned in 1930.

The roads weren't very good then. People still relied on riverboats to take them to Everett and the railroads to chug them out of town and deliver the mail. Both railroads operated their own depots then, the pair of them facing off across the tracks as if challenging each other.

But the boom times disappeared as fast as the huge old-growth trees in the hills. When the logs were gone, sometime just before 1920, so were the loggers who came down out of the hills to do business in town. The local economy stagnated.

In 1920, 258 people lived in Duvall, U.S. census counts show. Ten years later, the population numbered 200. By 1950, still just 236 people called Duvall home.

Without the timber economy of the past, local merchants relied on the loyalty of the dairy farmers who grazed and milked their cows in the surrounding meadows." It wasn't the farmers who made the town, but it was the farmers who kept the town alive," said Bob Kosters, a 75-year-old retired dairyman who moved to the area in 1940.

Still, Duvall maintained its charm. The farmers dealt with bankers who knew their names and their land. The merchants sold on credit. Folks knew each other and life chugged along like the riverboats that better roads had made obsolete.

"You could drive through the town with a team of horses and pull over and get some ice cream," Kosters recalled. About 1960, developers started dividing land into tracts and city folks found affordable homes outside the urban bustle. The population jumped from 345 in

DUVALL HISTORICAL SOCIETY

1960 to 607 in 1970.

Yet it was still an out-of-the-way, peaceful enough place that some 1960s "peaceniks" found rural bliss and stayed into the '70s. By 1980 the population was 729.

Then, with the boom in development on the Eastside, Duvall was discovered. By 1990, 2,770 people called Duvall home. Today the population is 4,238.

To old-timers like Kosters, things will never be the same.

"I loved to hear that old train whistle at night," he said.

"It used to be you'd see one car come through in a day. It's sad. Duvall's nothing big, but the history is very interesting."

CHAPTER 20

UNLOCKING THE LAKE

The lowering of Lake Washington brought unexpected changes to the Eastside

If things had gone differently, Kirkland's waterfront parks would be underwater.

The Hiram M. Chittenden Locks would be in downtown Seattle.

And steamships would cruise toward Lake Washington from close to where Safeco Field stands.

The changes would have come if different decisions had been made, if different business alliances had been formed or if different political viewpoints had prevailed in a venture that seems nearly inconceivable now.

The venture was building the Lake Washington Ship Canal, a task that resulted in dropping the water level on Lake Washington by 9 feet.

Towns and businesses were destroyed. In Columbia City and elsewhere, piers where boats had tied up led only to mud. An entire river disappeared.

While accounts differ, it's generally agreed that a connection between Lake Washington and Puget Sound first was proposed at a picnic on July 4, 1854, on the shore of Lake Union by Thomas Mercer, one of Seattle's most famous pioneers.

The reasons were based, as they often are, on money. While Seattle was developing along the shores of Puget Sound, timber, coal and other resources were waiting to the east. But getting there wasn't easy. Moving a load of coal from Issaquah to a ship on the Seattle waterfront required 11 cargo transfers from wagons to boats.

As with many ideas, the concept was easy. The execution was something else.

Alternative canal routes

Six options were considered for the Lake Washington Ship Canal at the turn of the century.

1 A Smith Cove route would have gone between Magnolia and Queen Anne Hill through to Lake Union.

2 Known as the Mercer Farm route, would have gone from Elliott Bay, along where Mercer Street is now, to Lake Union.

3 The Tramway route would have connected Elliott Bay to Lake Union near where Broad Street is now.

4 Would have run through Beacon Hill; Interstate 90 runs through the excavated gap where the canal was to go.

5 Would have followed the Duwamish Waterway and Black River, and entered Lake Washington from the south.

6 The final option, and the one that was chosen, goes from Salmon Bay to Lake Union and then to Lake Washington.

In 1869 another pioneer, Harvey Pike, tried to dig a canal through the Montlake area with a pick and shovel. In 1883 a group of businessmen built a small wooden lock in Fremont. And in 1885 a 16-foot-wide canal was dug between Lake Washington and Lake Union. But such rudimentary efforts were far from what was envisioned.

BY PEYTON WHITELY

Chittenden's solution

Proposals of the time described how Lake Washington would become a great naval harbor and fleets of commercial ships would anchor there, their hulls free of weeds in the fresh water.

Federal money was provided for an 1890 survey. Five routes were considered, providing a look at what might have been.

One route would have followed the Duwamish and Black rivers, and entered the lake from the south. Another, known as the Mercer Farm route, would have gone from Elliott Bay through downtown Seattle to Lake Union.

A path slightly farther south also would have connected Elliott Bay to Lake Union. Both central Seattle routes would have required double locks and land cuts hundreds of feet deep.

Another route would have gone between Magnolia and Queen Anne Hill to Lake Union. The final option went from Salmon Bay to Lake Union and Lake Washington.

A group of businessmen led by a former territorial governor, Eugene Semple, had its own plans: to dig a canal a mile long and 300 feet wide through Beacon Hill.

Hiram M. Chittenden

Semple gained the support of the Seattle Chamber of Commerce and other backers, and digging began in 1895. Lawsuits were filed, financiers pulled out, and work stopped in 1904. But the work helped create Harbor Island, and Interstate 90 runs through the excavated gap in Beacon Hill where the canal was to go.

The real action started when Hiram M. Chittenden arrived in 1906 as Seattle district engineer. Chittenden advocated a Salmon Bay route, said the locks should be built from concrete instead of wood and recommended the configuration of one large lock and one small one. He also recommended against having another set of locks at Montlake, concluding they could be skipped by allowing Lake Washington to fall 9 feet.

Political and business maneuvering followed, and in 1910 Congress OK'd spending $2.2 million to begin the canal.

Work started in September 1911 and took nearly five years to finish. The Ballard Locks opened in August 1916, and formal dedication took place July 4, 1917.

Eyesore on the Eastside

For the Eastside, the effects weren't what anyone expected.

Kirkland was the biggest city at the time, but most of the area was nearly wilderness. For years, the exposed lake bottom was an eyesore.

The East Side Journal, a weekly newspaper, reported in 1918 that flowers were being planted near the city ferry dock to transform the waterfront "from an unsightly spot into a beautiful flower garden." As late as April 1926, the paper reported that a builder, Guy Farrar, planned to develop a "Spanish village" along 2½ miles of waterfront. A few Spanish-style bungalows were built, but the project was never completed.

The town of Wilburton dried up when sawmill operators could no longer float logs to the mill.

The Ballard Locks did generate some shoreside activity, including the basing of a whaling fleet at Bellevue's Meydenbauer Bay and the development of

THE SEATTLE TIMES, 1913

Excavation for the locks was well under way at the entrance to the Lake Washington Ship Canal in 1913, two years after construction began.

MUSEUM OF HISTORY AND INDUSTRY

In 1916, as water from Lake Union's Portage Bay poured through the Montlake Cut, Lake Washington began to fall, losing 9 feet before the two lakes were level.

THE SEATTLE TIMES, 1917

The Roosevelt, Robert Peary's ship on his North Pole expedition in 1908-09, was the first through the Montlake Cut when the ship canal opened July 4, 1917.

shipbuilding at Houghton, where hundreds of ocean vessels were built and thousands of people worked during World War II.

But after the wartime boom, shipbuilding faded, and as late as the 1960s much of the Eastside's waterfront was viewed as second-class property, a place where oil tanks and creosoted piers were common scenes.

The lowering did have an unforeseen effect. Much of Lake Washington Boulevard, which became the main Eastside highway before Interstate 405, was built on the former lake bottom. It was the automobile, not shipping, that transformed the area.

How a river vanished

One of the most remarkable effects occurred at the south end of Lake Washington, where the natural outlet was the Black River, which drained into the Duwamish. About a mile from the lake, the Cedar River drained into the Black.

Early photos show a bucolic scene of lazy farms along the Black, but nature was far from benign. Almost annually, the lake would overflow, and the rivers would flood large areas of what's now Renton, Tukwila and the Green River Valley.

A 1911 flood was particularly bad, and in 1912 Renton dug a commercial waterway that moved the Cedar into a 2,000-foot-long, 80-foot-wide channel which moved the mouth of the river to the lake. Four years later, the ship canal was completed, and the Black River disappeared.

Joseph Moses, a Duwamish tribal member, later recalled what he saw then:

"That was quite a day, for the white people at least. The waters just went down, down, until our landing and canoes stood dry and there was no Black River at all. There were pools, of course, and the struggling fish trapped in them. People came from miles around, laughing and hollering and stuffing the fish into gunnysacks," he wrote.

The Ballard Locks were officially named the Hiram M. Chittenden Locks in 1956 and are one of Seattle's top visitor attractions, drawing 1.5 million people a year.

More than 80,000 vessels a year use the locks, 80 percent of them pleasure craft.

Miles of parks and the region's most expensive homes have been developed on what was once lake bottom.

This is how the Black River looked near Renton before 1916. When the Lake Washington Ship Canal was built, the lake dropped 9 feet, and the river disappeared.

Sources: "Renton, Where the Water Took Wing" by David M. Buerge; "Our Foundering Fathers" by Arline Ely; "Dig the Ditch" by Suzanne B. Larson; "The Lake Washington Story" by Lucile McDonald; "He Built Seattle: A Biography of Judge Thomas Burke" by Robert C. Nesbit; "Passage to the Sea," published by the Northwest Interpretive Association; "Tukwila, Community at the Crossroads" by Kay F. Reinartz; files of The Seattle Times and the Eastside Journal; and exhibits and other materials compiled by the Army Corps of Engineers.

CHAPTER 21

GREAT ESCAPES

The Eastside was the place to be on a sunny Saturday in the early 1900s

MARYMOOR MUSEUM OF EASTSIDE HISTORY

As a burgeoning city around the turn of the 20th century, Seattle was a hurly-burly of noise and pollution. Residents wanted an escape. And when they looked to the weekend, they looked to the Eastside.

Across Lake Washington, they saw a pastoral place that man had not yet cluttered — an area where nature had been given just enough of a civilizing touch, in the form of picnic grounds, dance floors and beaches.

And so they boarded ferries and came. Seamstresses spread lunches under shade trees at Meydenbauer Bay. Sailors and office clerks swam near modern-day Kirkland, then danced into the night along the shore. The affluent built vacation homes in places such as Medina and Enatai.

It was a stretch to elevate the beach resorts to "Seattle's Coney Island," as one touted itself, but the Eastside was the indisputable place to be on a sunny Saturday in the first half of this century.

Dozens of resorts, large and small, popped up during the years, from Mercer Island to Lake Sammamish and beyond.

Quick and easy

The steamboat and the railroad made getaways from the city quick and easy. Cable railways appeared about 1890; they could bring Seattleites to Leschi Park and Madison Street on the west side of Lake Washington, where they could board steamboats for scheduled rides around the lake.

At first, travelers stayed close to home, on Mercer

Construction of more and better Eastside roads gave weekend vacationers access to additional picnicking places.

BY CHRIS SOLOMON

Island. The Calkins Hotel, built in 1891 on the island's northwest side, was big and fancy, with 24 rooms, electric lights, indoor plumbing and a boathouse that could hold 100 small craft. It burned down in 1908.

A steamer line took daily trips around the island in summer, dropping the gang-plank at numerous favorite picnic spots. One was Fortuna Park near the present Shorewood Apartments by the East Channel bridge. Fortuna Park once boasted the largest dance hall on the lake, along with a bathhouse and fields for play and picnicking. Its heyday was from 1915 until 1920, though it may have been in business as early as 1909.

The east shore of the lake was slower to become a recreation destination. The few early Eastside hotels targeted business travelers and loggers, though one entrepreneur took advantage of the abundance of wild ducks on the Sammamish River and built a saloon and sportsmen's hotel near the north end of Lake Washington. Hunters rode the Seattle Lake Shore & Eastern Railway to reach the hotel from 1895 until 1905, according to local historian Richard McDonald.

Dance halls and picnic grounds eventually appeared from Kenmore to Bellevue — spurred by ferry operators who were looking for ways to boost weekend traffic.

Big bands, bigger parties

As early as 1906, one operator began to advertise excursions from Seattle to a leafy park above the eastern shore of Meydenbauer Bay in Bellevue. Called Wildwood Park, it became a place of big bands and bigger summer parties; crews would take the generator off the ferry after the last run and use it to light the dance floor.

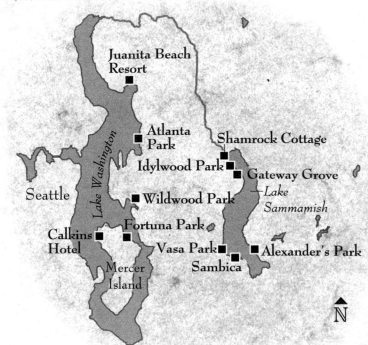

Eastside resorts

Juanita Beach Resort

Atlanta Park

Shamrock Cottage

Idylwood Park

Gateway Grove

Lake Sammamish

Seattle

Lake Washington

Wildwood Park

Calkins Hotel

Fortuna Park

Vasa Park

Alexander's Park

Mercer Island

Sambica

N

The annual Big Basket picnic, held in late July, was a Wildwood staple — "guaranteed to bring out more people than any other occasion," wrote Lucile McDonald in "Bellevue: Its First 100 Years."

Part block party, part county fair, the Big Basket promised such thrilling competition as the fat-men's race and ladies' nail-driving contest. The largest family that attended received five pounds of butter. The oldest married couple headed home with a slab of bacon.

The ferries eventually stopped using Bellevue as a port of call, and the stream of Seattleites almost dried

Juanita Beach Resort, touted in 1927 as "Seattle's Coney Island," lured visitors with its swimming pier, cabins and 5,000-square-foot dance pavilion.

MARYMOOR MUSEUM OF EASTSIDE HISTORY

up, too. After 1928, Wildwood's owners tried to reinvent it — the dance floor saw boxing matches and a roller-skating rink — before they let it fall into disrepair by the mid-1930s.

About the time Wildwood was in its heyday — 1916 — engineers completed the Lake Washington Ship Canal and locks. The lake dropped 9 feet. Suddenly, soft sand beaches appeared — and a pioneer family named Forbes took advantage of it.

For the 'common man'

The Forbeses' Juanita Beach Resort bloomed from a snack bar to a complex with swimming dock, cabins and a 5,000-square-foot pavilion for dancing; a 1927 ad called it "Seattle's Coney Island."

The resort was particularly popular in the 1920s, along with neighboring Shady Beach and Sandy Beach. Every night was Ladies' Night, with 25-cent admission for women; men had to pony up 50 cents. Visitors could rent swimsuits and beach towels, since neither was considered necessary to own in that era.

"They were resorts for the common man," said Richard McDonald in a recent interview. "They were usually family oriented. They were considered respectable places."

Some were more respectable than others. Not too far away at Houghton, in what is now Kirkland's south end, was Atlanta Park, where Prohibition booze was reputedly served and the clientele could get rowdy. Eastside mothers were known to ban their children from visiting Wildwood, too, since Monday mornings usually dawned on a few inebriates sleeping it off on the grass, too drunk to catch the ferry home the night before.

While most Seattleites who took the ferries were daytrippers, some of the affluent began building vacation homes in Medina, then Enatai, about 1915. Boatloads of guests would come across the lake to play and paddle at the waterfront homes of people such as Dr. James Tate Mason, of Virginia Mason Hospital fame. Moneyed bigwigs such as James Clise and the prominent Furth family also built estates.

On to Lake Sammamish

As time passed, the resorts on Lake Washington lost their luster. New ones, however, bloomed a few miles east on Lake Sammamish — aided by a railroad that skirted its eastern shore. By the 1930s, nine resorts crowded that lake, five on the northwest shore alone.

Resorts such as Shamrock Cottage, at the base of present-day Northeast 38th Street, did gangbusters business (particularly during Prohibition, when the taps kept flowing).

Dozens of rowboats and canoes drifted about the lake on bright summer days, while more people picnicked along the shore. The resorts offered cabins for longer stays. The Gateway Grove resort boasted a 22-foot high dive and a 40-foot steel water slide by the early 1950s.

Another resort with a big slide was Alexander's Park, on the lake's east side, which stayed in business from 1916 until 1985. The site ultimately met the fate

MARYMOOR MUSEUM OF EASTSIDE HISTORY

The Gateway Grove resort on Lake Sammamish tried to distinguish itself from competitors with Big Bertha, a 40-foot water slide built in the 1950s.

Sources include Eastside historian Richard McDonald; "Our Town Redmond," by Nancy Way; "Bellevue: Its First 100 Years," by historian Lucile McDonald; and Alan Stein, curator of "The Legacy of Eastside Parks and Gardens" exhibit at Marymoor Museum of Eastside History, which ran for several months in 1999 and 2000.

of others and was subdivided for homes.

On the southwest shore of Lake Sammamish, near present-day Interstate 90, nonprofit Vasa Park was built in 1926 by a Swedish cultural group and "was a great place to polka," wrote Nancy Way in "Our Town Redmond." Not far away, a Swedish church in 1919 built a Bible camp called Sambica.

By World War II, some 50 small resorts were sprinkled around East King County. One of the largest was Norm's, at Cottage Lake east of Woodinville. It had a staff of 40 and handled up to 10,000 visitors a day in the summer.

Many of these privately owned playgrounds closed in the postwar decades, about the time Eastside cities began to form.

Fortunately, many city parks departments saw the allure of the resorts. Norm's, Juanita Beach, Idylwood on Lake Sammamish's northwest shore, Wildwood on Meydenbauer Bay — these and others were eventually bought by cities or by King County and became public parks.

Some private residences eventually changed hands, too. Clise Mansion became part of Marymoor Park, and, in 1988, the grounds of the Furth summer home became the Wetherill Nature Preserve, a 16-acre habitat for natural flora given to Hunts Point and Yarrow Point.

With these acquisitions, local governments helped ensure that the Eastside remains a place where escape can still be found.

CHAPTER 22

THE GOLD COAST

With views of mountains and water, mansions abound

1888 PHOTO COURTESY OF ARLYS AND JACK GALE

Seattle newspaper publisher Leigh Hunt logged part of Hunts Point to clear a view for his mansion on Yarrow Point.

Long before microchips and the World Wide Web, when Northwest entrepreneurs made fortunes with trees, fish, gold nuggets and old-fashioned banks, Medina was already a Mecca for mansions.

The tiny town, and the nearby fingers of land jutting into Lake Washington's eastern edge, earned the moniker "The Gold Coast" decades before giants of the computer world, like Microsoft founder Bill Gates, built their palatial homes there.

By the roaring 1920s, mansions with man-made streams, pagoda roofs and carefully crafted grounds dotted the lake's edge. Men of fortune shot rounds of golf at the fledgling golf club.

"The splendor that the people with money lived in there was quite something," said Junius Rochester, a Seattle historian who is writing the history of one mansion. The arrival of industry magnates in the late 19th and early 20th centuries — at a time when much of the Eastside was forest and farmland — and their enduring presence now, is a vivid illustration of the real-estate agent's cliché: location, location, location.

BY WARREN CORNWALL

The Gold Coast sits closer to Seattle's business district than any other part of the Eastside, except Mercer Island. Before bridges joined Lake Washington's east and west shores, the Medina ferry dock was a hub for people looking for a quick trip to Seattle.

A 1913 newspaper ad heralded the arrival of ferry service that would carry people and their cars from Medina to Seattle's Leschi Park neighborhood in under 10 minutes. Medina residents could reach the Smith Tower, the symbol of Seattle's commercial aspirations, in 25 minutes.

"To the business man who wants a house in the country while he spends the day in the city, great vistas of opportunity are opened," the ad declared.

The coast also offered an escape from the crush of city life, and a heck of a view.

Mansions along the shore or perched on the bluffs above the lake had a panoramic vista of the lake, the setting sun and the hills of Seattle.

One early resident — Seattle Post-Intelligencer publisher and entrepreneur Leigh Hunt — wanted the view so much, he is said to have logged part of Hunts Point to get a better western look from his mansion on Yarrow Point, to the east.

Wordsworth inspiration

Hunt was perhaps the first Seattle magnate to erect a mansion along the Gold Coast, in 1888. His mark remains. Yarrow Point earned its name from his estate, which he titled "Yarrow" after an estate in poems by William Wordsworth. In addition to a close shave, the other tip of land also got its name from Hunt.

But he wasn't the first non-native to settle there.

Much of the area's forests were already felled by loggers and had given way to berry farms and fruit orchards, including the strawberries that became the focus of various Eastside festivals. In the 1870s, Seattle businessmen started snapping up some of the prime waterfront property.

The title of first permanent resident of the yet-to-be-named Medina fell to Seattleite Thomas Dabney. Around 1886, he laid claim to land on the southern tip of what is now Medina, built a dock there, and dubbed it "Dabney's Landing." Medina City Hall now stands

JACK FROST AND THE EASTSIDE HERITAGE CENTER

HARPER'S WEEKLY
Artist's drawing of a steamer on Lake Washington in 1891.

near that spot.

In the following decades, huge homes began to rise up along the shore. There was "The Gables" of Edward Webster, secretary and general manager of the Independent Telephone Co. in Seattle. Capt. Elias Johnston, a millionaire from the Yukon gold rush, bought land around Dabney's Landing in 1912 and built a mansion topped by a Japanese pagoda roof.

The area also gained a name, after a neighborly skirmish. Dabney favored the name "Flordeline." Another resident, Flora Belote, led a campaign for "Medina Heights," named after the Middle Eastern city that is Islam's second-holiest city.

A war of attrition ensued as each side took down the other's town sign and replaced it with its own, until Dabney eventually relented.

The Gold Coast moniker

The go-go days of the 1920s cemented Medina's reputation as a home for the wealthy.

A real-estate campaign begun in 1919 by Johnston and William Calvert pitched the area as "the heart of a charmed land."

A decade later, the area, while not yet a city, could count among its residents publisher Miller Freeman; James Clapp, whose family was closely tied to the Weyerhaeuser timber company; and William Neal Winter, head of the Everett Telephone Co.

People could golf at the new Overlake Golf Club and celebrate the annual Strawberry Festival at the Clapp mansion, complete with a man-made stream that flowed into the lake. The stretch of shoreline had, by then, earned the "Gold Coast" moniker.

Jack Reynolds, one of the longest continuous residents of Medina, recalled the splendor of these homes with their soaring staircases and beautiful wood detailing.

"You should have come over and seen these big colonial mansions," the 88-year-old marveled from the porch of the Medina home where he has lived since 1942.

Cars traveled from the Medina ferry dock to Seattle's Leschi Park neighborhood from 1913 to 1940.

David Hagenstein, left, and his son, Walter, ran the Medina Grocery from 1910 to 1950. The grocery closed in 2000.

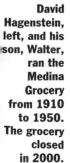

JOHN FROST AND THE EASTSIDE HERITAGE CENTER

His presence in the town shows the area wasn't just a playground for the rich. When he bought his house for $2,000, he worked as a welder in the Seattle shipyards. Later, he became a maintenance man at the power plants of Puget Power.

In the middle of the 20th century, Medina still had a flavor of country living. Reynold's land included an orchard of cherry and apple trees. He kept a Jersey cow, rabbits, chickens and turkeys across the street from some of the town's big estates.

A fear of losing that quiet setting helped prod the small communities along the Gold Coast to finally turn themselves into official towns.

The opening of the Lake Washington Floating Bridge in 1940 jump-started growth on the Eastside, as families went looking for suburban living still a quick drive from Seattle.

Cities incorporate

Seeking to control their own fate and fend off encroaching development with home-grown regulations, Medina and Hunts Point incorporated in 1955, followed by Yarrow Point in 1959.

Legal walls, however, couldn't freeze time in the cities.

Reynolds watched with part sadness, part astonishment, as at least one of the town's landmark homes was torched in a training exercise for local firefighters. Others were torn down.

In their places rose new, bigger houses. The most

The new and the old: Bill Gates' waterfront estate in Medina is in stark contrast to Bill Lebrick's pioneer cabin near 76th Avenue Northeast and Northeast 28th Street.

Golfers teed up for a tournament at Overlake Golf and Country Club.

THE SEATTLE TIMES, 1966

breathtaking: Gates' 43,000-square-foot home.

Other residents in 2002 include former Microsoft president Jon Shirley, Amazon.com chief Jeff Bezos and Costco Wholesale co-founder Jeffrey Brotman.

The mansions of old are giving way to the mega-mansions of barons of the new economy.

HARLEY SOLTES / THE SEATTLE TIMES, 2001

JACK FROST AND THE EASTSIDE HERITAGE CENTE

Sources include "A Point in Time: A History of Yarrow Point, Washington" edited by Suzanne Knauss; "Lakelure: A Tale of Medina, Washington" by Junius Rochester; and "Kemper Freeman, Sr. and the Bellevue Story" by Robert F. Karolevitz.

CHAPTER 23

WOODINVILLE

A neglected graveyard in the middle of the city is a link to a forgotten past

"(There were) just big stumps all around here when I grew up and big tall snags that hadn't been logged . . ."

Elmer Carlberg, Woodinville historian who called himself "Son of the Stumpland."

At center: Susan Woodin and her daughter Mary

Harp-shaped fencing that once surrounded Woodinville's cemetery was replaced years ago with chain link. At the graveyard entrance, weeds poke through a fountain's crumbling stone where water once gurgled in from Bear Creek.

The fence and the fountain, a white pergola that is still there and a grape arbor that isn't, were built by Elmer Carlberg. For 40 years the silver-bearded man, who wore a black trench coat and brimmed hat regardless of the weather, tended the town's dead in Woodinville Memorial Park.

Carlberg, a familiar sight until his death in 1987 at age 93, was a visible link to the history he took pains to preserve.

The son, grandson and great-nephew of early pioneers, Carlberg now rests a dozen paces from the graves of the city's namesakes, Ira and Susan Woodin. The Woodins donated an acre of their homestead for the graveyard in 1889.

In the middle of a growing city, the cemetery is nestled in the northwest corner of Northeast 175th Street and Woodinville-Snohomish Road. The flower beds Carlberg planted are overgrown with weeds, and litter is strewn among headstones.

While motorists zoom by oblivious of its existence, the burial ground is one of the last reminders of a time when virgin cedar was prime currency, front parlors doubled as community centers and settlers transformed the valley into farms.

Sammamish village at the mouth of Bear Creek

Woodinville's rolling hills, rivers, lakes and ponds were carved out more than 14,000 years ago by the retreating Vashon Glacier. For generations before the area's early Norwegian and Danish immigrants arrived, a Sammamish Indian village was at the mouth of Bear Creek, above what is now Northeast North Woodinville Way.

At least 100 people lived there, fishing and traveling along the Sammamish River, farming root and bulb crops, and hunting and gathering throughout the watershed.

Ira Woodin, his wife, Susan, and their two daughters became the first white family to settle in the area,

arriving in 1871 after two bachelors had established homesteads.

Woodin was a New York native and a partner in Seattle's first tannery and shoe-manufacturing business. His wife was born in Oregon's Waldo Hills.

They packed up their home in the Columbia City area, crossed Lake Washington by scow and slowly traveled up the Sammamish River, then called the Squak Slough, to their 160-acre homestead. The old Woodin home on Northeast Woodinville Drive was torn down in the early 1950s.

Susan Woodin, then in her 20s, rowed across Lake Washington twice a month to sell butter in Seattle. For years she walked the three miles from Madison Park landing to Seattle and back again. She couldn't afford the stage, but a driver she

Woodinville Memorial Park, shown here about 1920, is one of the city's few remaining historic sites.

WOODINVILLE HISTORICAL SOCIETY

BY SARA JEAN GREEN

This was Woodinville about 1905, viewed from an old wooden bridge across the Sammamish River. Principal buildings were the hotel, left, the Hansen barn, a school-desk factory and a general store, the white structure.

befriended carted the butter to Seattle while she walked.

The Woodins weren't alone in the wilderness for long. Emmanuel Neilson, a Norwegian, and his daughter Mary settled on land adjacent to the Woodins in 1876. Neilson later built a grocery and hotel on the site.

Mary eventually married a Danish carpenter named Anders Hansen. She plotted most of the lots in Woodinville, and her husband built homes for new settlers. She deeded part of her family's homestead for railway lines and a highway in the 1880s, according to grandson John Halver, 77, who was born in an apartment above the old Neilson grocery.

Four other families — the Jacobsens, Petersons, Bargquists and Calkins — also came to Woodinville in the 1870s.

A social center

From the 1880s onward, as more homesteaders and loggers moved into the area, the Woodin home became something of a halfway house between Seattle and upriver settlements. The social center of the new community, Susan Woodin's front parlor hosted the first school, Sunday school and church services. The Woodins later built a grocery, and Susan Woodin became the town's first postmistress.

Woodinville got its first church in 1880, built across from land that later became the cemetery, and a one-room school house three years later. A two-room school was built in 1902 but burned in 1908. A brick schoolhouse — the only one in King County outside Seattle — was built a year later on the site where

Woodinville's City Hall now stands.

Although the commercial district began along Northeast Woodinville Drive on the south bank of the slough, it moved across the river after the the railroad arrived in 1888, the same year Elmer Carlberg's parents came to Woodinville.

By 1909, Woodinville had two sawmills, two shingle mills, several groceries, four hotels, a railway station, a blacksmith's shop, a feed store, a stage-coach operator, a brick and tile manufacturer, and a small school-desk factory.

From 1909 to 1911, Fred Stimson, a wealthy lumber baron, built Stimson Manor as a vacation home on the grounds now occupied by the Chateau Ste. Michelle winery. Stimson owned a prize dairy herd, greenhouses and a lighted tennis court and often

The Hollywood Schoolhouse was built in 1912. Materials were donated by lumber tycoon Fred Stimson.

entertained large groups of people from Seattle. Eventually sold, the house became a speakeasy during Prohibition and is listed on the National Register of Historic Sites.

The area known as Hollywood Hill, which got its start as the Derby logging community, was renamed around 1911 at Stimson's prompting. He requested the name change after he lined his long driveway with holly trees. Stimson then bought more land on Hollywood Hill for a poultry farm that employed dozens of locals.

"They kept building more and more chicken houses and their employees increased," said Helen McMahon, a longtime resident and charter member of the Woodinville Historical Society.

Arthur Heidedorf, who eventually bought the 200-acre ranch, cross-bred his poultry and established hatcheries in Japan, Brazil and Germany, she said.

Soon after, the Hollywood Fox Farm started up, raising fox and mink for their pelts.

As Woodinville's stumpland was cleared, dairy farmers and vegetable growers began taking advantage "of some of the richest soil in the state," McMahon said.

1950s bring changes

The rural landscape of Woodinville began to change in the 1950s when people started moving east from Seattle and other areas, drawn to the pastoral lifestyle within commuting distance of the big city.

Horse ranches became more popular, and Egon Molbak came to Woodinville in 1956 and opened a nursery that now draws a million customers a year.

Most of the town's early pioneer homes were razed in the 1950s and '60s to make way for brick buildings.

Development began in earnest in the 1970s, and

WOODINVILLE HISTORICAL SOCIETY

whole neighborhoods popped up on prime agriculture land, transforming Woodinville into a suburban community.

Growth accelerated in the mid- and late 1980s when Woodinville Towne Center, fast-food restaurants, video stores and other retail businesses set up shop along Northeast 175th Street.

Woodinville became a city in early 1993 and now has more than 10,000 residents, with thousands more living in nearby unincorporated areas.

Despite the growing population, 19 people have been buried in the Woodinville cemetery since 1990. The historical society's Gladys Berry said many residents are unaware of it, instead choosing their final resting place in other cities.

"But I'm reserving my plot and one for my husband," Berry said, leaves crunching underfoot as she pointed to an anvil that marks the grave of blacksmith Johann Koch. "This is where I want to be, surrounded by my town's history."

The community's two-room schoolhouse was built in 1902 and burned six years later. A brick school was erected at the site in 1909.

Sources include "Village in the Woods," edited by Suzi Freeman, Gloria Kraft and Linda Packard (1993); "Squak Slough 1870-1920" by Amy Eunice Stickney and Lucile McDonald (1977); and the Woodinville Historical Society.

CHAPTER 24

MEYDENBAUER WHALERS

Bellevue was one of the last active whaling ports in the United States

Bellevue was a rural backwater when American Pacific Whaling moved its headquarters and winter berth to Meydenbauer Bay in the early 1920s. Here, the fleet awaits the next season.

WILLIAM LAGEN COLLECTION / BELLEVUE HISTORICAL SOCIETY

I n the decades between the world wars, seven steam-powered boats, their high bows weighted with harpoon cannon, rode out winters tied two and three deep to a lonely wooden pier that reached into Meydenbauer Bay.

No one could have known it at the time, but Bellevue's quiet, crook-fingered bay on Lake Washington was where the nation's long tradition of whaling would come to an end.

For much of the 1920s and '30s, this alcove was home and headquarters for American Pacific Whaling and a family that for a time dominated commercial whaling in the Pacific Northwest.

By the time the company folded in the 1940s, Bellevue was one of the last active whaling ports in the United States.

Of steam and noise and whales

Few people are left who can recall the steam and the noise and the weather-worn men converging on Bellevue's waterfront each year when the small fleet of whaling boats prepared to leave for a season of har-

pooning blue, sperm and humpback whales in Alaska.

What remains today of the company's pier and warehouse now belongs to the city. Bellevue bought them in 1998 as part of the Meydenbauer Bay Marina, which eventually will become a park.

It seems certain the city will dedicate at least a portion of the marina to recall Bellevue's days of whaling.

Whether it warrants much more is a matter of debate. The company's reach stretched across the icy waters of the North Pacific but left a relatively small mark on the city.

Except for a few hectic days in spring and fall — when the fleet was readied for another season, and

BY J. MARTIN McOMBER

again when it returned rusted and worn — the boats were more of a quiet curiosity than anything else.

Only a few people worked year-round for the company. The sailors, the gunmen, the flensers (who stripped the blubber), the cook, the oilmen and the other 150 or so whalers and workers mostly vanished for the winter, many of them to bars on Seattle's Skid Road.

Still, William Schupp and his seven boats were about the biggest thing going in Bellevue when his company moved its headquarters to Meydenbauer Bay in 1919.

Peder Oness, right, and Alfred Pedersen, longtime captains for American Pacific Whaling, fit an explosive point on a harpoon aboard the Kodiak, circa 1935. The Kodiak was one of several whalers that wintered in Meydenbauer Bay.

Locks made it possible

Schupp was a Michigan native who had made a fortune in the insurance industry before he began building a whaling empire with the purchase of American Pacific Whaling in 1915.

It was a search for a freshwater winter port for his steel-hulled fleet that brought him to Bellevue, which then was little more than a few hundred people, farms and a couple of stores along Main Street.

The newly built Ballard Locks in Seattle had opened Lake Washington to the sea, and Meydenbauer Bay was perhaps the most protected spot on the water. Kirkland's shipyards — where the boats would be hauled out each spring for repairs — lay just a few miles north.

Bellevue was never a place where the hundreds of whales slaughtered each year were hauled from the water, stripped of their blubber and meat, then rendered into oils, food and fertilizer.

That task was saved for the company's two whaling stations at Port Hobron and Akutan in Alaska, places you could smell long before you could see them.

But in March, the wooded hillsides of Meydenbauer Bay would begin to echo with the sounds of ships being made ready for the season's hunt.

Chipping hammers rang as paint and rust were stripped from the topsides. There was the smell of hot tar as the men slathered it on the lines and rigging and decks.

By mid-May, after the boats had returned from being overhauled in Kirkland, they were loaded heavy with supplies, food, harpoons, exploding tips and fathoms and fathoms of sturdy manila rope.

Some motley crews

Then the crews would begin to arrive. Most of the men were immigrants, many of them from Norway. A lot looked like they had just come off a three-month drunk or three months in jail. Some looked as if they'd done both.

But all the men were ready to spend the next five months on a boat or a desolate island, with no radio, no

Worn from a season's work up in Alaskan waters, the Tanginak and the Moran wait out a 1920s winter in Meydenbauer Bay, harpoon guns mounted on the bow.

American Pacific Whaling was headquartered in Bellevue, but its fleet hunted and processed whales at two stations in Alaska. Here, workers begin the task of flensing a humpback whale.

WILLIAM LAGEN COLLECTION AND BELLEVUE HISTORICAL SOCIETY

entertainment, little to do and less to read.

Good jobs were difficult to come by, especially during the Depression. And whaling paid at least $30 to $40 a month, food and lodging included.

On sailing day, the boilers would be lit, and steam that drove the boats' engines would begin to build. And when it was time, the men climbed aboard and the boats peeled away from the dock for the weeklong trip to Alaska.

"Getting under way was a time of smoke, steam, tearful farewells and ... great excitement," recalled William Lagen, who, as Schupp's grandson, grew up around the whaling fleet in the family home above the pier.

The end of the hunt

But that excitement waned in the 1930s. The fevered hunt for whales began to take its toll.

The catch numbers fell. So did the demand for whale products as the world's economy slumped.

It was the war with Japan that finally put an end to American Pacific Whaling's work. The Navy halted whaling in Alaska, and the boats were refitted for military patrols.

Schupp tried to revive the business after the war, but he died unexpectedly in 1948.

The pier — no longer alone on the bay — changed with the times.

Bellevue in the 1950s began to bloom as a haven for middle-class families seeking a home in the suburbs. Soon William Lagen turned his grandfather's dock into a marina.

Pleasure boats replaced whaling boats, and the city moved on to different pursuits.

Sources include the Bellevue Historical Society.

CHAPTER 25

BEFORE THE BRIDGES

Until 1950, most Eastsiders crossing Lake Washington traveled by ferry

SEATTLE TIMES ARCHIVES

When you ride a tour boat from Kirkland's Marina Park, it's easy to wonder what it would be like to take a ferry from Kirkland all the way across Lake Washington to Seattle. Such a trip used to be commonplace. For more than 80 years, ferries were the chief way to cross the lake.

The Leschi, built in 1913, carried riders across Lake Washington for nearly four decades.

At the peak of service before World War I, dozens of small ferries stopped at countless docks around the lake — hence the term "mosquito fleet." They serviced sizable communities such as Kirkland and Bellevue as well as family docks, with ferries operating more like taxis than scheduled buses.

In a memoir of the steamer Dawn, a 55-footer built in 1914, Madelon Moore Konker tells of runs made from Leschi to Eastside stops named Lake, Merrimount, County, Franklin, Zimmerman's, Alymore's, Proctor and Thompson, and to private docks — including one where a woman always got on board in her bathrobe and finished dressing on the ferry.

It's been nearly 50 years since the last lake ferry offered scheduled passenger service.

That ferry, the Leschi, made its final run from Madison Park to Kirkland Aug. 31, 1950, with Capt. Frank Gilbert at the wheel. That day, he turned over command to Merle Adlum, who took the Leschi to a Vashon Island run.

It later became a cannery vessel and sank in Alaska.

One person who saw the Leschi on Lake Washington was Frank Rosin, who grew up along the Kirkland lakefront near the ferry dock.

"I watched it make its last run across the lake with a tear in my eye," recalls Rosin, who was 15 then and fondly remembers the cross-lake trips. "It was exciting to me."

People would play cards on the 20-minute crossing, he recalled, and a woman named Olga Dunkle ran the lunch service.

BY PEYTON WHITELY

A horse and carriage waits with an auto to board a ferry at Bellevue's Meydenbauer Bay landing on Memorial Day 1914.

THE SEATTLE TIMES, 1914

Customs of the time separated the seating areas by gender, with women congregating on the north side and men on the south side, where they could smoke.

But the cross-lake ferries were not always filled with such pleasantness. Histories describe plots to thwart competition, battles over who would run the routes, continual struggles over money, and a collapse that finally came as tolls were removed from the Mercer Island floating bridge.

"Think of it, a full load on the Leschi was equal to the number of people crossing the floating span in 10 seconds during rush hours," wrote ferry Capt. Robert Matson in a 1990 history of the lake ferries, published by the Puget Sound Maritime Historical Society.

The golden years

Boat travel on Lake Washington originally involved canoes and rowboats, but the first power vessel was a craft named the James Mortie, which arrived in 1870.

Other boats followed, but service got a considerable boost in 1890, when a developer named Charles Calkins built a resort on Mercer Island, named it "East Seattle," and had a 74-foot craft built for the run from Leschi. Named the C.C. Calkins, it was launched March 21, 1890.

A young man named John Anderson was quarter-master, and by the time he was 22, he'd become captain. It was Anderson who would largely guide the future of cross-lake ferries.

Born in Sweden, Anderson went to sea as a cabin boy and arrived in Seattle in 1888. By 1892, he was able to acquire a half interest in a 52-foot steamer named the Winnifred for $1,500.

The Winnifred soon was making runs to Newcastle and carrying dancers on moonlight excursions, but the boat burned at Leschi in August 1894. Anderson used the insurance money to buy an 80-foot ferry boat named the Quickstep.

Anderson was adept at moving the boats up the Black River at the south end of Lake Washington, pulling them over sandbars at high water to reach the lake; the river and the route disappeared when the Ballard Locks opened in 1917 and the lake's level was lowered.

Anderson discovered there was a strong market for excursion cruises, and began running a yacht named the Cyrene around Mercer Island in 1903, with money from the cruises providing a major part of his financing for decades.

In 1906, many of the lake runs were combined under the name of the Anderson Steamboat Co., with Anderson as president.

The ferry terminal at Seattle's Leschi Park around the beginning of the 20th century.

SEATTLE TIMES ARCHIVES

Anderson also excelled as a ship-builder, first operating a shipyard in Seattle near Leschi and later moving it to what is now the site of Carillon Point in Kirkland. The first vessel built there, the 95-foot Atlanta, was launched in 1908.

Anderson's timing was perfect. By 1909, the year of the Alaska-Yukon-Pacific Exposition at the site of what now is the University of Washington, Anderson was running 12 boats.

"That was the golden year of steamboating on Lake Washington. For 30 years, Anderson was an important figure on the lake," reported the late Lucile McDonald, a local historian, in one of her books, "The Lake Washington Story."

Around the turn of the century, a controversy over public and private ownership developed. King County began to run a ferry, named the King County of Kent, from Leschi to numerous Eastside sites.

But the vessel seemed to be jinxed, getting stuck in a mud bank at her launching in 1899. The county ended up losing about $100,000 a year on the lake operations, according to the 1983 book "Ferryboats: A Legend on Puget Sound," by Mary Stiles Kline and George Bayless.

After years of fighting, Anderson was appointed King County superintendent of transportation in 1919. By 1921, the county had lost so much money the routes were put out for lease, and Anderson took over the lake routes.

In 1922, Anderson expanded his cruises, taking as many as 300 riders at a time on the lake and Puget Sound.

"Anderson recognized that most of his money on Lake Washington had been made, not by providing ferry service, but by providing pleasure cruises and sightseeing tours," wrote Kline and Bayless.

Fighting the bridges

Paved roads were already becoming a threat to lake travel, and what would prove the ultimate threat was being discussed. In 1929, the Marine Digest reported that talks were going on at the Frye Hotel in Seattle about building a bridge across the lake.

Bridge talk faded with the 1929 stock-market crash, but was revived by 1939. That January, King County canceled Anderson's lease on the Lake Washington ferries as the state and county moved to build a floating bridge to Mercer Island. Anderson fought the bridge. A lawsuit ensued and was settled out of court.

The Mercer Island bridge opened in 1940; Anderson died in May 1941.

The Madison Park-Kirkland run continued for about 10 years after the bridge opened, with the city of Kirkland appointing operators. The run was successful during World War II, when shipbuilding was booming at the Houghton shipyards.

But ridership fell after the war, and came to an end after tolls were removed from the Mercer Island bridge in 1949. At that time, the Leschi was carrying about 1,500 riders a day.

On the Leschi's last run, a Seattle Times reporter, Robert Heilman, reported that Gilbert, the captain, "seemed to avert his eyes," and his chin trembled as he handed over control to Adlum.

In July 1950, the East Side Journal, a weekly newspaper in Kirkland, reported on Page 1 that talks were under way for a second lake bridge, and that a traffic survey was being done.

At the time, some 19,000 vehicles were crossing the Mercer Island bridge daily, and "20,000 to 37,000 is considered capacity," the paper noted.

The Evergreen Point Floating Bridge opened in 1963. Now each lake bridge carries more than 100,000 vehicles daily.

J.H. Bligh of Kirkland pays his fare to Robert Matson. Bligh's car was the last to board the Leschi on its farewell trip Aug. 31, 1950.

CHAPTER 26

MERCER ISLAND

The island's rich history includes Native American folklore and colorful pioneers

ALLA OLDS LUCKENBILL GARRISON / MERCER ISLAND HISTORICAL SOCIET

S haped like a footprint without toes, Mercer Island stretches about six miles long in the southern half of Lake Washington, just four miles across at its widest point.

A drive around this once-isolated tree-covered hump reveals little of the history that transformed it into today's upscale, tightly knit community. But for those islanders who look hard enough or reach back far enough to their own roots, the island is still rich with clues and memories that link today's residents to the island's history.

The Indians

In the distant past, the Snoqualmie Tribe had two villages on the west shore of Mercer Island, south of today's Interstate 90, but nothing is left of those villages.

What is known is that the Snoqualmies frequented the island to fish and gather berries and to meet for potlatches with the Duwamish and Suquamish tribes.

Charles Hinzman, the wife of Mary Anne Hinzman, Snoqualmie tribal secretary, remembers that when he was growing up on the island in the 1930s he could walk along the shore near the former village sites and pick up coffee cans full of arrowheads and even stone hatchet heads.

"There were only a little over a thousand people living there then, scattered all over the island," he said.

The white pioneers

Mercer Island was named after one of the Mercer brothers — Thomas, Asa or Aaron — who came to Seattle in the 1850s and 1860s, but historians don't

An 1890 photo shows Charles Olds, left, and his family at thei home on the east side of the island. Or the right are Agnes Olds and daughter Alla, wearing a hat, and son, David. Also shown is part of the orchard, which gave the home-stead the name Apple-ton.

BY LOUIS T. CORSALETTI

The luxurious Calkins Hotel, pictured here as it burned in 1908, was built in 1890 by pioneer C.C. Calkins. Calkins had earmarked the west side of Mercer Island as a resort and town called East Seattle. He eventually went broke on the hotel project — which included sprawling gardens, fountains, Turkish baths and a 100-slip boathouse — and it changed hands several times before the fire.

agree on which one. None of the brothers ever lived on the island.

It is known that Judge Thomas Mercer, the oldest of the three brothers, was friendly with local Native Americans and often had an Indian row him from Seattle to the island in the morning and return in the evening to row him back. Mercer is said to have enjoyed picking berries and walking along the shoreline.

The first federal government survey, made in 1860, named the island Mercer's Island.

Aaron Mercer, who came to Seattle with Thomas, filed a claim on Mercer Slough in Bellevue, which today bears his name.

Asa, the youngest of the trio, is best known for traveling back to the East Coast and bringing two groups of "Mercer Girls" to Seattle, in 1864 and 1866, to marry the large number of single men.

The first permanent settlers, Charles and Agnes Olds, made the island home in 1885. Within five years there were 15 families on the island.

David Garrison said one story sticks in his mind about his great-grandfather, Charles Olds, who apparently got along with Native Americans who visited the island after whites settled there.

"They often would leave fish at his doorstep, without any great ceremony," he said.

It was C.C. Calkins who, after arriving in Seattle in 1887, put Mercer Island on the map.

After buying a chunk of land on the west side of the island he built his fabulous Calkins Hotel and platted what he hoped would become a town called East Seat-

tle — a name for that neighborhood that remains today.

He then built an ostentatious brick home on Calkins Point, now the site of Luther Burbank Park. But Calkins went broke, and family misfortunes plagued him until he left the area and never returned.

Another colorful pioneer was Alla Olds Luckenbill Garrison, who arrived with her parents in 1885 and spent her life on the site of the former 160-acre Olds family farm until her death in 1955.

Charles Olds felt that higher education was "wasted" on women, but Alla Garrison challenged her father and went to the Territorial University in Seattle. She supported herself by working as a domestic in private homes.

In retaliation, her father sold her horse. When she returned to the island to teach at the East Seattle School in the late 1890s she had to walk the 10-mile round trip from Appleton (the Olds Farm) to the school every day.

Delores Echinger, who has lived on the island since the 1930s, knew Alla Garrison as a "cantankerous benevolent," recalling that the hardy pioneer would often row from the Olds farm to the south end of the island to bring food to a needy family.

During World War II, Alla Garrison allowed soldiers from two anti-aircraft-gun installations on the island to come to the farm to ride her horses.

A member of the Woman's Christian Temperance Union, she was active in island affairs until her death.

The bridges

For almost four decades, island residents relied on small ferries to travel to and from the mainland. Finally, in 1923, the first East Channel Bridge was opened, connecting the island from Barnabie Point to Enatai in Bellevue.

The 1,200-foot-long bridge allowed the 2,500 island residents to drive to Seattle via Renton.

By the 1930s, the old wooden structure was so rickety that children on school buses heading to and from the island to Bellevue got out and walked across the span, and another bus picked them up on the other side. Under President Franklin Roosevelt's Work Projects Administration (WPA), a new bridge was built.

The Lake Washington Floating Bridge, linking the

Abandoned in the mid-1920s, the Briarwood wharf once stood on the east shore of Mercer Island, across from Beaux Arts Village. The wharf was used by steamboats and other boats on the lake until King County stopped operating lake craft in 1921.

The original East Channel Bridge connected Mercer Island and the eastern shore of Lake Washington in 1923, giving island motorists a route to Seattle via Renton. This view is looking east.

WASHINGTON STATE DEPARTMENT OF TRANSPORTATION

island and the entire Eastside with Seattle, was opened in July 1940 and later renamed the Lacey V. Murrow Bridge in honor of the state highway director who was active in its realization.

Two municipalities

Newcomers to the area don't realize that about 30 years ago there were two local governments on Mercer Island, the result of a decades-long head-to-head battle over what sort of local government was to be established.

An election in 1945 to incorporate the island divided residents and the proposal was defeated. Over the next 25 years it was a free-for-all:

•November 1953: Voters turned down incorporation or annexation to Seattle.

•July 1960: Voters in the area generally south of what is now the central business district approved incorporation of the city of Mercer Island.

•August 1960: Voters in the area along what is now I-90 voted to incorporate as the town of Mercer Island. Over the next decade there was much debate over merging the two entities.

•May 1970: Voters throughout the island approved a merger of the two municipalities as the city of Mercer Island.

Schools

Shortly after settling on the island, Charles Olds saw the need for a school and with George Miller, who lived at Enatai across the East Channel, drew up a plan.

The island's first school was a former one-room cabin in the area called Briarwood, near what was to become the island end of the East Channel Bridge.

Only the Olds children and other island students would attend school at Briarwood for four months. Then classes were held for Miller's children and others at Enatai for four months.

Olds and Miller hired Henry Kelsey, recently arrived from New York, as the teacher, and he moved back and forth from the mainland to the island for his teaching assignments.

Next came the East Seattle and Allview schools in 1889, followed by McGilvra and Lakeview.

Until 1955, when Mercer Island High School opened, older students had a choice of going to Bellevue or Franklin high schools. The first graduating class was in 1958.

Sources include "Mercer Island Heritage" by Judy Gellatly, published by the Mercer Island Historical Society.

CHAPTER 27

WAR COMES HOME

World War II brought jobs, an influx of people and a preview of future prosperity

MARYMOOR MUSEUM OF EASTSIDE HISTORY

A s viewed from the sky, the Eastside was dark at night during World War II, but it was a lively time on the ground.

A huge shipyard in Kirkland worked around the clock building warships, then emptied thousands of workers into waiting dance halls and taverns. Civil-defense patrols watched for enemy planes and other signs of invasion, while households canned, sewed and recycled to help the war effort.

And lights were doused at night to hinder a potential aerial attack.

Lake Washington Shipyards was bustling when this photo was taken in 1945. The site is now Kirkland's Carillon Point.

"Strange it was to look across the lake not to see any light, Seattle was all blacked out, a city that had advertised itself as the best lighted city in the world," wrote Mercer Islander Alfred Fleury in memoirs kept at the Bellevue library.

As it did across the country, the war gave the Eastside economy a jump-start after the Depression. Prosperity helped people cope with worries, fears and tragedies.

Events during the war years of 1941 to 1945 also pushed cities east of Lake Washington toward their suburban destiny, but that's not what springs to mind when locals are asked about that time.

People pulled together

Eastsiders remember working hard, pulling together and finding ways to get by despite the rationing of food and gas and dwindling supplies of household goods. Several said life wasn't all bad despite the horrible events taking place overseas.

BY BRIER DUDLEY

"Maybe you couldn't have a gallon of gasoline or coffee or sugar, maybe you had to wait to get what you needed, but we didn't suffer," said Jennie Bryden, 86, of Redmond.

Bryden's family ran a trucking business, so they had gas. The problem was finding drivers, since most able-bodied folks joined the service or took factory jobs.

One employee who stuck with the Brydens was Daryl Martin, now 80, who was turned down by the military because of a head injury. Martin worked in the office and drove when nobody else was there.

Martin also inspected tires for the rationing board, and at night played in a dance-hall orchestra. He spent several hours a week at the observation tower downtown watching for enemy planes.

"There would be times when we'd hear about a sub off the coast, or what they were doing in Alaska and how long would it be before they were here, but it got to where you took it in stride," he said. "We had enough to worry about with family members in the service."

Bryden said coping with rationing wasn't difficult because many people had a few acres on which they could grow some food or keep chickens or livestock.

Farms on the Eastside were encouraged to boost production, but there was a desperate shortage of labor.

Internment pain widely felt

Making it worse was the loss of Japanese-American farmers. In the spring of 1942, all people of Japanese descent in the Eastside area were put on trains in Kirkland and sent to internment camps in California, Idaho and Montana.

Altogether, 443 were sent from the Eastside, including more than 300 from Bellevue.

With 95 percent of the berry farmers interned, Bellevue canceled its annual strawberry festival, although the official reason was that gas was in short supply.

Other Eastside businesses prospered during the war. A turkey cannery and compass company grew in Bellevue, but the biggest changes were in Kirkland, where a Navy contract transformed Lake Washington Shipyards and the city.

For years, the small private shipyard had maintained ferries and fishing boats. But the Navy needed new ships fast, so it bought land and

DIANA SCHAFER FORD / BELLEVUE HISTORICAL SOCIETY

expanded the Houghton complex to the east and west. It also gave the company machine shops, ramps, cranes, a dock and a cafeteria.

Workers came from around the country; by war's end, the company payroll had grown from 250 people to 8,000. Through the war they built 29 Navy ships, mostly seaplane tenders and torpedo motherships, and repaired 477 ships, including some from Britain and Russia.

Suddenly people had money to spend; new businesses opened to fill the need. Merchants reported their best Christmas season ever in 1942, but prices were rising and giving locals an economics lesson.

First taste of inflation

"We went from a depression into a war," Martin said. "You're thinking, boy, you've got a raise and another 20 bucks, then you go into a store and you wonder where it went because everything went up. That was our first taste of inflation."

The surge of workers from across the country also clogged streets, filled every rentable living space and overwhelmed Kirkland's sewer system.

In 1942, residents were asked to register available beds; the next year, rent control was imposed because landlords were gouging defense workers.

Martin, who played saxophone at dances, recalled shipyard workers coming straight to the parties.

Winifred Evans Schafer and Violet Cort Schafer cover their ears during an air-siren drill in Bellevue in this 1945 photograph.

"They'd dude up the best they could before going to work, then take off their aprons and coveralls and go right to the dance halls," he said. "They really whooped it up. When it comes to playing, my lips looked like somebody hit me."

Officially Kirkland had about 3,700 residents by 1945, but the post office estimated it was serving 17,000, including temporary defense workers and their families.

Three huge housing projects opened to accommodate workers, and a new sewer system was built, but not all the problems were solved. With parents on the job, juvenile crime and shoplifting increased. The pro-

jects and taverns were often rowdy, a gambling ring booted from Seattle came to Kirkland, and the city had to buy another jail wagon.

Some residents were so fed up, they fought efforts to keep the Navy work after the war.

That momentous decision killed Kirkland's last chance to become the smokestack city envisioned by its founders, and the shipyard closed around 1970. It was used as the Seattle Seahawks' training facility, then was destroyed by fire in 1979.

In 1989 the shipyard site reopened as Carillon Point, where today yachts glisten in place of grimy warships.

---

*This story includes material researched by University of Washington graduate student Alice Promisel.
Other sources include Lorraine McConaghy of the Museum of History and Industry in Seattle; "Bellevue: Its First 100 Years,"
by Lucile McDonald, 1984; "Kemper Freeman, Sr., and the Bellevue Story," by Robert Karolevitz, 1984;
"Mercer Island, the First 100 Years," by Judy Gellatly, 1977.*

THE SEATTLE TIMES, 1947

Construction of Bellevue Square, looking much different from today, began in mid-1945.

FROM BARGES TO BELLEVUE SQUARE

The Eastside's future actually was changed by two shipyards, the one in Kirkland and Olympic Shipbuilders in Port Angeles.

The latter gave Medina resident Kemper Freeman Sr. the capital to build a shopping center called Bellevue Square.

Freeman had won a wartime contract to build wooden barges and started the Port Angeles shipyard. But it apparently had trouble getting lumber, and the barges were late. It also didn't perform as expected, and in 1943 the contract was canceled after just four of eight barges were delivered.

Freeman protested, and with help from then-U.S. Rep. Henry M. Jackson, he received a settlement that "provided him with enough capital to permit contemplation of new investments," according to a history book on Freeman sponsored by the family.

At the time, defense paychecks were giving Kirk-

land merchants record sales, but Bellevue had few attractions.

Freeman and his father began buying land and chose to build a shopping center on a farm east of Main Street.

The government authorized Freeman to use precious lumber for the center's first building, the Bel-Vue Theater, because it would improve morale on the homefront.

One impetus was a War Manpower Commission study that found defense workers were leaving Bellevue as soon as they could, partly because there was little to do in the sleepy farm town.

Work began on the theater in mid-1945, a few months before Japan surrendered.

The center helped fulfill the dream of a prosperous suburb that civic boosters envisioned when the floating bridge to Seattle opened in 1940.

CHAPTER 28

EASTSIDERS IN EXILE

More than 400 local Japanese Americans were sent to internment camps

WIDE WORLD PHOTO, 1943

Before he was forced to leave Bellevue for a California internment camp, Mutsuo Hashiguchi wrote a letter to "lifetime buddies, pals and friends," and left it with the town's newspaper.

"With the greatest of regrets, we leave you for the duration, knowing deep in our hearts that when we return, we will be welcomed back, not as pariahs but as neighbors," wrote Hashiguchi, then chairman of Bellevue's Japanese American Citizens League.

"This is not a letter of goodbye, but a note saying — au revoir."

Hashiguchi kept his word, returning with his family to their Bellevue home after World War II. But for most of the 400-plus Japanese and Japanese Americans who lived on the Eastside in the 1930s and early 1940s, the wartime evacuation was a permanent goodbye to the area — and a very painful one.

"One day in May, these children were gone," says Pat Sandbo, recalling when the three Japanese-American students in the second-grade class she taught were taken from Bellevue. "It was just very upsetting. It seemed at the time that it was very sudden."

Executive Order 9066

About three months passed between President Franklin Roosevelt's signing of Executive Order 9066 — authorizing the evacuation and internment of about 110,000 people of Japanese descent from the West Coast and the departure of the Eastside's Japanese and Japanese-American population.

During that time, Tosh Ito, then 19, remembers being required to stay within a 35-mile radius of his home and having government-imposed curfews. Others recall their families' frantic preparations as they tried to figure out how to store their possessions (they were each allowed to bring only what they could carry) and how their farms would survive.

Bellevue had 472 acres of produce farms cultivated by Japanese immigrants and their descendants. Families also farmed in the Rose Hill and Juanita areas of Kirkland. They had felled 200-foot trees and dynamited stumps 5 feet in diameter, on land once considered unfarmable, to grow lettuce, peas, cauliflower, beans and celebrated strawberries.

"Our parents had worked so hard clearing the stumps," recalls Mitzie Hashiguchi, Mutsuo's widow. "I think it was hardest for them."

"Wartime hysteria"

After Japan's bombing of Pearl Harbor on Dec. 7, 1941, the federal government decided that West Coast residents of Japanese descent were a security threat. The government didn't officially acknowledge until 1988 that this assumption was groundless, and that the internment was motivated by "racial prejudice and wartime hysteria."

At the time, an editorial in the Bellevue American suggested that local Japanese-language schools be discontinued.

A year after Executive Order 9066, Japanese and Japanese Americans toil in the fields of Tule Lake, Calif., site of the nation's largest internment camp.

BY JANET BURKITT

"You have friends who respect your industry, your thrift, your support of local and national drives," it said. "We wish to deal fairly and respect your rights. But we will always remember Pearl Harbor."

Many issei, the first generation to immigrate to the Eastside, and their children, nisei, who were U.S. citizens, tried to convey their patriotism.

Three weeks before Pearl Harbor Day, 46 Eastside Japanese Americans bought $1,875 worth of defense bonds. Eastside nisei, among other Japanese Americans, later served in the war.

Still, rumors spread that Japanese American farmers in Houghton and Medina planted their 1942 crops in coded patterns for Japanese bomber pilots, according to a thesis by Lorraine McConaghy, a historian with the Museum of History and Industry.

Signs posted by the government in early May told Japanese and Japanese Americans they had to move in two weeks, but the signs said little else.

"I didn't know where we were going, or when we'd be back," recalls Mitzie Hashiguchi. "'We hope to see you someday,' That's all we could really say," to white people in the community.

Sandbo remembers a feeling of helplessness among many white Eastsiders, too.

"I think people just felt . . . that this was one of those things that happened, and that as loyal Americans, they had to accept it, even though they thought it was very unfair," she says. "I don't think anyone thought they could protest."

Letters from the camps

Some students skipped school May 20 to watch as roughly a quarter of Bellevue's population was forced to leave. One-fifth of Bellevue High School's class of 1942 had to put off future plans; nearly all of Bellevue's berry farmers were forced to leave behind their harvests.

They boarded railroad cars in Kirkland as guards stood by with bayonets. The blinds in the cars were drawn, and the passengers were not allowed to raise them.

They traveled overnight to Pinedale, Calif., where they would live in a detention center — one small room per family — for the summer, sleeping on cots

E-33-Apt.5
Pinedale, Calf.
May 25, 1942

Dear Miss Groves,

I arrived here May 20, 1942 after a very nice train ride. The soldiers and porters were very nice and polite Pinedale is very pretty. We saw our first orange tree. It is very hot here but I am getting used to it. the day we came here we had to boil the water before we drank it. I have lots of fun with other boys but I wish I was back home. I hope you have a nice picnic. Please write to me

very truly
Dick Kodani

Pat Groves Sandbo's second-grade class at Bellevue's Main Street School lost three students in May 1942. Sue Suguro, front center, and Dick Kodani, back center, wrote to their teacher about their experiences.

PAT GROVES SANDBO / BELLEVUE HISTORICAL SOCIETY

with straw mattresses they stuffed themselves.

Later, they would be sent to the Tule Lake, Calif., camp, where they faced similarly grim conditions. Still, Sandbo's students in the camp tried to be cheerful in replies to their classmates' letters.

"It is very hot here but I am getting used to it," one boy wrote from Pinedale. "The day we came here we had to boil the water before we drank it. I have lots of fun with other boys but I wish I was back home."

Their parents, of course, grasped the injustice of

their situation. And the news they heard from the Eastside often wasn't good.

Families learned that their houses had been burned down or ransacked, some within days of the involuntary evacuation.

White families storing their friends' valuables were the targets of such acts, too.

Many white Eastside residents did help their Japanese and Japanese-American neighbors and friends during the war. "There was a lot of sympathy," Sandbo recalls.

And there was a lot of racism: One prominent resident was quoted in the press about the "hyphenated loyalties" of his former neighbors, and described a 1930s Japanese plot to export its citizens to the United States as part of a "Pacific conquest," McConaghy wrote.

When Bellevue got word that internees were being released, 500 signed a petition demanding that people of Japanese descent not be allowed back in the city. Some businesses said they would not cater to Japanese or Japanese-American patrons.

The Hashiguchis were among roughly 15 to 20 families who returned to the Eastside. Many who didn't return had nothing to come back to: The Alien Land Law of 1921 prohibited most issei from owning land, so many prewar farmers had grown their crops on leased property.

Most who did return found their land in disrepair and did not continue to farm for long.

Kiyo Yabuki, who was wounded in battle in southeastern France, counts his family fortunate to have had friends who took care of their property during the internment.

Still, some people refused to buy the produce they grew when they returned to the Hunts Point area.

Some whites did welcome their fellow Eastsiders back, as Hashiguchi predicted.

"The students that went to high school with me were so happy to see me again," recalls Mitzie Hashiguchi. "People came out of the woodwork to help us get back on our feet again."

But the Hashiguchis also found their greenhouse

THE SEATTLE TIMES, 1945

windows smashed, their carefully stored valuables taken and their house destroyed. Dead animals and garbage filled their well, their only source of water.

"Everything was stripped — just demolished," she says. "It took a long time to fix."

Pfc. Kiyo Yabuki, front, and his brother Hideo work in their fields in Bellevue in August 1945.

Sources include The Eastside Japanese American History Project; the Densho Project; the Bellevue Historical Society; "The Lake Washington Shipyards: For the Duration," by Lorraine McConaghy.

CHAPTER 29

CELEBRATIONS

Eastsiders have always known how to throw a good party

BOTHELL HISTORICAL SOCIETY

It was the Fourth of July, 1886, and the party was at Dave and Mary Ann Bothell's farm in the town that would be named after them. A dance floor was constructed in the cow yard, and local fiddlers Bill Johnson and John Bittinger had the crowd on their feet. Settlers from Houghton, Juanita and all along the Sammamish River had gathered to celebrate the nation's 110th birthday.

A Fourth of July parade in 1907 crosses the Sammamish Slough into Bothell. Norway Hill is in the background.

Several miles to the south in the coal-mining town of Newcastle, other neighbors were celebrating in a style that would bring the police out today: shooting pistols in the air and setting off dynamite.

The Eastside has always known how to party.

Dozens of celebrations once considered annual have come and gone over the past century. Still others continue.

Issaquah's once-popular rodeos were reined in by advancing suburbia. Bellevue's original Strawberry Festival was a casualty of World War II. Organizers rolled up Kirkland's too-popular Moss Bay Celebration just a decade ago.

The Pacific Northwest Arts Fair, meanwhile, has hung around Bellevue Square for half a century, and Salmon Days in Issaquah has been hatching fishy jokes and spawning crowds for 29 years.

"Humans need to celebrate life," says Salmon Days coordinator Robin Kelley. "If you go back in history, every community has had a celebration about something, be it harvest or crops."

Some parties were impromptu, such as Bothell's

BY SHERRY GRINDELAND

bonfire bash celebrating construction of the Lake Washington Ship Canal early this century. Upper Sammamish Valley residents celebrated because the canal would lower Lake Washington and eliminate rainy-season floods.

Other events existed because they were well-orchestrated and an opportunity to bring money, customers and would-be residents to town.

Restaurateur Carl Pefley organized the first Bellevue arts and crafts fair to draw attention to the new Bellevue Square shopping center. Charles Bovee, one of the men behind Bellevue's original Strawberry Festival, owned Bellevue Realty.

The festival put the town on the map, according to The Reflector, Bellevue's newspaper of the time. In its second year, 5,000 strawberry shortcakes were sold. In the third year, visitors came by boat and in 500 cars.

The event would survive until the World War II internment of Japanese farmers, ending the strawberry production.

Bothell, platted in 1889, has been home to numerous festivals. Its Fourth of July parade, which dates to the turn of the century, is the longest-running on the Eastside.

THE SEATTLE TIMES, 1946

Two other Bothell festivals ended for safety reasons. One was a motorcycle climb on Norway Hill; the other featured speedboat races on the Sammamish Slough. Boats started at Lake Washington, raced to Lake Sammamish and returned to Lake Washington. Fewer than half the starters ever finished.

Salmon Days and pig races

An early Issaquah event, the city's traditional Labor Day parade, hung around until 1969. Started in 1936, the community celebration featured such entertainment as rolling-pin throws and "husband-calling."

Today's big event in Issaquah is the annual Salmon Days Festival. Started in 1970 to celebrate the salmon returning to spawn, the festival attracts more than 200,000 people each fall.

Salmon have long been celebrated on the Eastside. Before settlers arrived to log the forests and farm the fields, Native American potlatches and celebrations held at various encampments, including near Marymoor and Snoqualmie Falls, featured salmon. In 1955, the Fall City Derby Days included an evening salmon bake prepared by Makah tribal members from Neah Bay, along with the traditional parade and races.

One of Kirkland's more memorable but short-lived celebrations occurred in 1946, when community festivals were sprouting after the end of World War II. The main attraction was a pig race in Lake Washington. Margaret McDonald recalls how she and other young women were part of the show.

"They tied a barge up at the end of the dock and had chutes on the barge. The pigs were sent down the chutes, into the water, and we girls had to dive off and follow them in to shore," McDonald said. "Nobody got hurt, but the pigs were frightened."

McDonald and her sister Martha Mallar have vivid memories of the 1930s annual kids parade in Kirkland.

Pigs are flying at the start of a swimming derby at a Kirkland summer festival.

Charles Kelly, left, and Harold Kelly pay tribute to the 1946 queen of Bellevue's Strawberry Festival, Patricia Henry.

THE SEATTLE TIMES, 1941

Children dressed in costumes and marched in the parade, winning prizes for the best costumes. But Mallar said the most exciting part was after the parade.

"We would got to the old Gateway Theater, and businessmen gave us each a bag of hard candy, an orange and a free ticket to the movies," she says. "It was a big deal in those days."

Success killed the Moss Bay Celebration, which started in 1972 and continued until the late 1980s, and was dubbed Kirkland's annual traffic jam. The end came when city organizers realized that more people were arriving after the festival closed at 9 p.m. than were leaving. "Various bars in town were beginning to have problems," said Doris Cooper, who was mayor during several of those years. "It was time to stop."

Another longtime Eastside festival, Redmond's Bicycle Derby Days, started in 1939 when downtown businessmen wanted to raise money to purchase flags for the city sidewalks. They invited bicyclists to race the 25-mile route around Lake Sammamish.

One year a Redmond resident and bike rider stopped at a prearranged spot, put his bike into a boat and rowed across the lake. His early finish surprised serious racers who didn't find his practical joke all that funny.

Woodinville residents seem to have the best sense of humor about their festivals. Their past rodeos and motorcycle races have been replaced with Celebrate Woodinville, including such festivities as an annual April Fool's parade and Basset Bash that attracts hundreds of basset hounds and their owners. In recent years, wine festivals have included a grape stomp.

FESTIVALS PAST AND PRESENT

Bellevue

Strawberry Festival: This ran from the 1920s through 1941; it was revived by the Bellevue Historical Society in 1987 as a small, community celebration.

Peter Puget Festival: In the 1980s this community celebration, honoring an early explorer, included a golf tournament and carnival.

Pacific Northwest Arts Fair: Started in 1946, this three-day fair attracts about 300,000 visitors annually.

Bothell

Fourth of July Parade: Bothell has celebrated Independence Day with a community parade since before the turn of the century.

Sammamish Valley Pioneer Picnic: This festival, started in the 1920s, still occurs each July.

Bothell Arts Festival: Started in the 1970s and continues each August with family activities, juried arts and crafts and food booths.

Fall City

Fall City Days: By 1955, what had started as a logging show was called Fall City Derby Day and included a salmon bake and torchlight parade of Native American canoes on the river. It's still an annual event.

Issaquah

Labor Day celebration: This ran from 1936 until 1969.

THE SEATTLE TIMES, 1958
Potter Stan Healea of Moses Lake displays his craft at Bellevue's Pacific Northwest Arts Fair.

Wild West Rodeo: The 1924 festival was the first one on record. Coal miners had set aside what is today's Memorial Field for community events, including ball games and a track for chariot and rodeo races.

Salmon Days: What started in 1970 as a small community event is now one of the Eastside's largest festivals.

Kirkland

Moss Bay Celebration: Started in 1972, it was ended by organizers in the late 1980s.

Kirkland SummerFest: Kirkland revived the downtown festival in recent years.

North Bend

Trout Days: A fishing derby and trout fry were held from the 1920s through the 1950s. They were replaced by a jamboree that featured equestrian events.

Alpine Days: Started by community supporters to match the alpine facade adopted by downtown buildings, this festival was held in the 1970s.

Redmond

Derby Days: The bicycle race, still running each July, started in 1939.

Heritage Festival: A three-day celebration around the Fourth of July has been held in Marymoor Park since the 1980s.

CHAPTER 30

CARNATION

Hundreds of dairies thrived for decades and brought renown to this remote town

At first they came with a few cows each, hard-working dairy families whose small barns popped up all along the Snoqualmie River Valley, their modest pastures emerging as they cleared the tree-studded land to make way for hay.

They milked by hand into buckets, poured it into cans and hauled the cans to horse-drawn carts or onto barges that were tugged down the river to the creameries and condenseries.

Soon there were dozens of farms, followed by bustling towns built largely on the dairy economy. One city even took its name from a big dairy just outside its boundaries.

Carnation Milk Farm
Near Carnation, Washington

"We had fresh milk all the time — and cream," recalls Isabel Jones, a lifelong Carnation resident and local historian. "Dairying was really our deal. Just about every place between Fall City and Carnation and Carnation and Duvall were all farms."

Those days are long gone, and so are most of the hundreds of small family dairies that once dotted the valley — victims of changing landscapes, changing economics, changing times.

"Now I think we have two dairies between Fall City and the Snohomish County line," Jones laments. "It's changed a lot."

But a century of dairy farming in East King County has left an indelible stamp on practically everything here — the history, the landscape, the people. Indeed, the history of the valley is, to a large degree, the history of dairy farming.

Pioneers found rich valley for growing

At the beginning of the 1900s, dairying was mostly a small, local affair, but pioneers found a rich valley for growing their enterprises.

Elbridge Amos Stuart

"This is an ideal dairy area because of the climate," said Dave Owens, a lifelong dairyman and now general manager of the Nestlé Regional Training Center, which used to be Carnation Milk Farms. "It's mild in the summer and mild in the winter. It never gets too hot; it never gets too cold."

With transportation and access to a large market difficult, farmers milked their cows for their own families or to supplement the incomes they made from raising other livestock and crops.

But advances in technology would soon change that.

A major contributor was Elbridge Amos Stuart and his new evaporated-milk company, Carnation, which was founded in 1899 and recently celebrated its centennial. For the Snoqualmie Valley, the company's large processing plant, built in Monroe in 1908, would be most important.

"All the dairies would take their cans down to the river, and the little boat would come and pick it up," Owens said.

Stuart bought a small dairy in the Snoqualmie Valley, a few miles outside of present-day Carnation and

Carnation Milk Farms is shown in a 1920s postcard.

BY IAN IITH

NESTLÉ REGIONAL TRAINING CENTER

Some of Elbridge Amos Stuart's first Holsteins are unloaded from a barge after floating downriver to his new Carnation Milk Farms about 1910. The breeding farm would become world famous.

began building his soon-to-be-renowned breeding farm, home to the "Contented Cows" made famous by decades of advertising campaigns.

"He shipped offspring all over the world," Owen said. "This farm became famous worldwide for its breeding stock, and the Carnation name became famous worldwide."

At its peak, the farm had 1,500 acres, nearly 1,000 head of dairy cattle and 129 employees — most of whom bunked on site. Before Nestlé bought out Carnation in 1985 and scaled back the operations, the farm also was a development center for pet and livestock food — and home to 350 dogs and 500 cats.

Tolt becomes Carnation — for a bit

Stuart's influence would help put a little town on the map.

It started in 1912 as Tolt, an enclave on the river with the same name, a hub for all kinds of business of the day, from dairying to logging to hops growing. When the railroad came through a few years later, things really took off.

"We were a booming town," said Jones, who was born in town in 1923. Her father, William Larson, was the town's first fire chief. "We had lots more businesses than we do now. There were two barbershops, three grocery stores, a bakery, a Ford car agency, hotels."

Come 1917, though, Stuart, a master of marketing and advertising, persuaded city leaders to change the name from Tolt to Carnation.

Carnation frequently boasted about its "contented cows" and the Snoqualmie Valley's dairy climate. This ad is from 1912.

"He said if it was Carnation it would put us on the map," Jones said. "It put him on the map, anyway."

Carnation loyalty lasted until 1928, when nostalgia

for the old Tolt name and some resentment about being manipulated by the now-huge company set in. Locals voted to go back to Tolt.

Still, locals reveled in the farm's national notoriety. Dignitaries came to the farm from all over in 1928 to unveil the statue of Holstein Segis Pietertje Prospect, whom everyone called "Possum Sweetheart," which set the record for producing the most milk of any cow ever. The statue still stands. Movie star Jackie Cooper once came all the way to Carnation just to crown a cow called Daisy after she set a world's record.

Even without the glitz, the company infused the town with support.

"It was great," said Jones, who was Tolt High School student-body president in 1941. "The Stuarts did a lot for us here in Carnation. Carnation Farms really worked a lot with our kids. We had all kinds of school activities, all our 4-H activities."

Eventually the tide shifted back in 1951, and the town became Carnation again.

Meanwhile, the dairy industry was to change forever.

In 1950, there were 12,000 farms and 240,000 dairy cows in Washington, according to government figures. In 1989, the number of farms had dropped to 1,300. As of November 2002, there were 628.

But on those fewer farms, there still are a total of 260,000 cows, producing more milk than ever. In fact, dairy farming challenges apple production as the largest agricultural producer in the state.

But in King County, urbanization has meant a decline in dairying in the Snoqualmie Valley and other regions. From 21,600 dairy cows in the county in 1991, only 15,100 remain today.

Beyond urbanization, there are a host of other reasons for the change in dairy farming: It's more efficient to run big farms. Environmental restrictions make it hard for small farms to operate. And while the price of feed, machinery, manpower and other dairy expenses keep going up, the price of milk has not risen enough to offset those costs.

NESTLÉ REGIONAL TRAINING CENTE

Movie star Jackie Cooper, in the trench coat, came to Carnation in 1936 to help crown Daisy, a Holstein that set a world record for milk and butter production.

"The direction of the whole dairy industry is just going to get bigger and get more efficient," Owens said. "You've got to milk more cows, but you have to limit your acreage. Dairies have a hard time keeping up."

It's not just a local problem. Nationally, between 1992 and 1996, 38,500 dairy farms shut down. Wisconsin lost 13,000 farms in the past decade — 2,000 just in 1998.

And Carnation is changing along with the times. It's not a hub for dairy farmers anymore. Carnation, like its neighbors north and south, is fast becoming a bedroom community.

"The days of the family farm are over," said Holly Thompson, another Nestlé spokeswoman. "Especially when I can work for Microsoft and make three times as much."

Sources include "The Carnation Milk Farms: Home of Contented Cows," edited by Robert D. Moore, and "Carnation, The First 75 Years: 1899-1974" by John D. Weaver.

CHAPTER 31

GETTING ON THE MAP

The desire to cross Snoqualmie Pass led to the creation of many Eastside roads

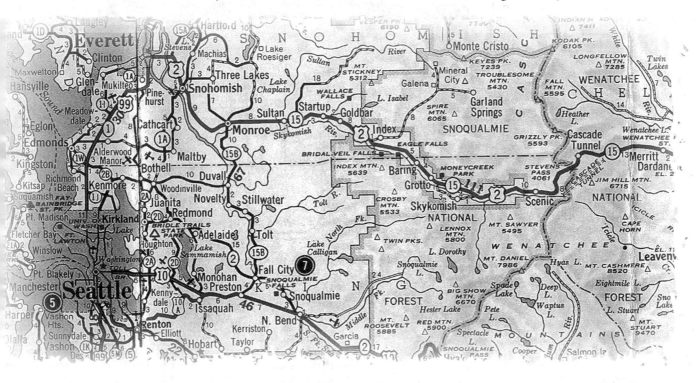

The maps are brittle now, creased and yellowed as they're unfolded, revealing a view of the past that's remarkable because of what's not there.

"Compliments of Hotel Mayflower" is stamped on one map, while an ad along the edge urges drivers to stay at the Shady Glen Auto Camp, 8600 Bothell Way.

There's no Interstate 405, no Interstate 90, no Highway 520.

There's no such place as Bellevue on this 1949 map by the H.M. Goushá Co.

A 1949 map given away at a Chevron gas station, shown at left, lists local cities and populations, with Kirkland at 2,084 people. Bellevue isn't shown; it didn't incorporate for four more years.

Now sold as collectibles in antique shops, the maps provide a glimpse of how the Eastside has been shaped by dramatic changes in transportation.

Just west of Fall City, for example, a building that housed a gas station in the 1920s still stands, its pumps gone but its facade intact, with the same owner since 1949.

Orland Hodges, 78, says he bought the station mostly for the blacksmith shop out back rather than the gas pumps in front.

"Five or six cars would come by in the morning on the way to the mill" at Snoqualmie, he said. "Then there'd just be one or two more all day."

A few other vestiges of life before congestion remain.

Sections of the "Red Brick Road" that once formed the main route to Yellowstone Park still exist in Redmond and Bothell. A 1920s trestle is part of Kirkland's Juanita Bay Park.

Bothell has opened a small park to memorialize a one-fifth-mile stretch of brick roadway, with signs explaining how, before the bricks were laid in 1913, going to Seattle required a six-hour boat ride.

BY PEYTON WHITELY

Another stretch of aging roadway runs alongside I-90 where the old Snoqualmie Pass Wagon Road winds down from Alpental Road at the summit. A water trough used to refill Model-T radiators still sits beside the road.

It was the desire to cross Snoqualmie Pass that led to many of today's Eastside roads.

"This has been the one pass through the mountains which our people have been ready and willing to plead for, to fight for, and to spend money for at any and all times," wrote Clarence Bagley in a 1929 history of King County.

Getting to the pass meant a trip of several days. Eastside historian Lucile McDonald told of settlers arriving in what is now the Bellevue area in 1885 and finding an "impassable barrier" of brush and 200-foot trees.

Ten years later, only about a half-dozen main Eastside roads existed, mostly mud covered with logs, and including what is now Northup Way and Main Street in Bellevue.

The office of the state highway commissioner was created in 1905, and by 1916 King County proudly reported it had 54 miles of paved road.

The first attempt to bring state control to road building was the creation of the Washington State Good Roads Association in Spokane in 1899. Its original 14 members included W.W. Perrigo of Redmond and Lee Monohan of Renton.

ASAHEL CURTIS

A four-horse hitch with a freight wagon travels the old Snoqualmie Pass Wagon Road during the late 1800s.

"There was not one state highway centralized power in all our states" until then, a 1939 history recounted. "These roads were built by the local political power, with no plan, system or purpose beyond the convenience of the municipality known as counties."

By the 1920s, Lake Washington was encircled by roads, with Lake Washington Boulevard reaching Bellevue from the south in June 1920.

The first car crossed Snoqualmie Pass in 1905, although it would be 1931 before the pass was open in winter.

Road building then was cause for celebration. A 1939 opening of a "superhighway" between Bothell

Kirkland's main drag was a lot quieter in 1925. This photo was taken at the intersection of what is now Lake Street and Kirkland Avenue. One sign points to the Seattle ferry.

THE SEATTLE TIMES, 1925

THE SEATTLE TIMES, 1940

The opening of the first Mercer Island floating bridge on July 3, 1940, draws a crowd to the Seattle end of the span.

and Seattle, now Lake City Way Northeast and Bothell Way Northeast, was marked by a parade, soap-box derby and street dance.

In 1937 the state Highway Department took over what had been a county road running roughly where 116th Avenue Northeast runs now, designating it Secondary State Highway 2-A. Twenty years later it would be picked as the route for I-405.

Over those years, the quest for better connections from Seattle to the east continued, resulting in the key event in Eastside transportation history: opening of the Mercer Island floating bridge in 1940.

One of the bridge backers was a publisher named Miller Freeman who saw it as a way to get crops from Eastern Washington to Seattle. A son, Frederick Kemper Freeman, was born in 1910, and worked with his father in publishing, built ships in World War II and became interested in real estate.

Kemper Freeman Sr., whose son, Kemper Freeman Jr., continued to develop Bellevue Square, was able to make the right land deals, and in June 1945 ground was broken for a 560-seat movie theater, the first building in what would become Bellevue Square. "Bellevue Square was designed to cater to those who cherished the freedom of mobility which the automobile afforded," wrote Robert Karolevitz in a 1984 biography.

In 1956 the federal interstate-highway system was approved, and by 1957 the state was expecting to spend $62 million on freeways in the next two years.

The Evergreen Point Floating Bridge opened in 1963.

Jammed in a cardboard box at the new state-archives repository at Bellevue Community College, a 1966 state traffic-lane study gave a view of the expected future.

"It seems obvious that even with six lanes on 405, an additional north-south facility still will be needed for the 1985-1990 projected traffic," the study found.

It calculated that 26 freeway lanes would be needed to carry the projected 160,400 cars a day.

By 1968, those dreams were fading. A plan to build a freeway from Auburn to Bothell through Lake Hills was dropped after 200 people showed up to oppose it.

Eastside mass-transit systems also failed, with the last independent Eastside bus system, Metropolitan Transit Corp., merging into Metro in 1973.

The last ferry run to Kirkland ended in 1950. A new I-90 bridge was opened in 1993 after 30 years of disputes. No second north-south freeway was built on the Eastside.

In 1997, I-405 carried an average of 141,400 cars every day at Northeast Fourth Street in Bellevue.

CHAPTER 32

FARM COUNTRY

Family plots thrived until postwar growth replaced them with roads and homes

Mitzie Hashiguchi keeps old photographs of a Bellevue farm where she and her father, Haruji Takeshita, grew strawberries on land now occupied by Coca-Cola and Safeway distribution centers. In the decades before World War II, Takeshita's family and seven other Japanese families farmed on the Midlakes-area property around 120th Avenue Northeast and Northeast 15th Street.

Japanese and Japanese-American families made up the bulk of berry farmers in the city and a sizable minority in prewar Bellevue.

Today the surviving members of those and other Eastside farm families are the last reminders of a diverse and flourishing agricultural region that has all but disappeared.

Before it became a land of cul-de-sacs, car-pool lanes, malls and minivans, the Eastside was known as farm country.

Drafty barns etched the skyline long before shimmering office buildings. Family homesteads dotted the landscape from Woodinville to North Bend. Dairy farms clustered in the Snoqualmie Valley between Duvall and North Bend. Fruit, vegetable and bulb farms blanketed what is now downtown Bellevue.

More than 70,000 acres of farmland were being worked in King County at the end of World War II, and much of that land was concentrated on the Eastside.

Fifty years later, that number was nearly halved.

Today developers in Bellevue build $400,000 homes on soil originally cleared for berries, beans and livestock.

As a teenager, Ewing Stringfellow and his father raised beef cattle and boarded horses on property along 140th Avenue Southeast near Main Street, across from where Sammamish High School now stands.

When the family bought the 48-acre lot for $320 an acre in 1949, the future already seemed bleak.

"All the farmers were down in Issaquah then. Bellevue farmers were fast becoming history," Stringfellow said. "People were coming down on Saturdays to see my dad to ask him if he'd sell the property."

It took 20 years of convincing, but Stringfellow's dad eventually sold the farm in pieces, starting in 1968.

The farm's ruins now stand side by side with condominiums, houses and an elementary-school campus.

Japanese presence

As the farms disappeared, so, too, did the dozens of immigrant families that had cleared and worked the wooded expanse between Lake Washington and Lake Sammamish.

Often the immigrant farmers cleared and cultivated land owned by white families because laws were designed to prevent immigrants from owning property.

The Takeshitas were among the few who owned their own land. In 1919, the Takeshitas, with help from a Japanese-American attorney, purchased 13 acres at Midlakes, where they grew strawberries, peas, tomatoes and cauliflower.

Hashiguchi eventually took over the farm for her

This 1930s family photo shows the 13-acre Takeshita farm, left, in the Midlakes area of Bellevue. The farm was purchased with the help of a Japanese-American attorney in 1919.

BY TYRONE BEASON

aging father, but by 1942, the war had foiled the family's success. About 65 families from Bellevue joined the thousands of Japanese and Japanese Americans who were sent to detention camps in California and Idaho.

Only 20 or so families returned to the Bellevue area. The land-owning Takeshitas were among them.

Hashiguchi, however, came home to an overgrown field and unturned soil. The farm suffered from neglect.

"It was a struggle — it was no paradise coming back to that field," Hashiguchi said.

The few remaining Japanese farmers, strapped for profits, started selling their increasingly valuable property to developers. The Takeshita family sold Haruji Takeshita's dream to the Great Northern Railroad in 1953.

Produce capital

The fine glacial soil around Bellevue was ideal for raising berries and other crops, a fact attested to on the labels of locally produced preserves and other goods.

William and Elva Sydnor's blueberry farm, in what is today the heart of downtown Bellevue, produced fruit grown on rich "upland soil" from 1931 to 1944.

"They're sweeter," boasted labels for preserves from Sydnor's Blueberry Farm.

R.T. Reid raised cherries, grapes, apples, pears and other crops on his farm, in what's now Bellevue's Surrey Downs neighborhood.

In 1925, the Island Belle grapes raised on Adolph Hennig's 8-acre farm at Northeast 21st Street and 100th Avenue Northeast commanded 10 cents a pound, "a good price," Hennig reported in a periodic review of his farm's performance.

Berry production was so closely associated with the region that from 1925 to 1941, thousands of out-of-towners flocked to Bellevue for the annual Strawberry Festival.

The dairy farms

Today wine and music flow freely at the Chateau Ste. Michelle Winery in the Hollywood neighborhood of south Woodinville. But in its earlier life, the old Hollywood Farm was a highly regarded milk producer.

Seattle lumberman Fred Stimson built the chateau as a summer retreat. Later he turned the 206-acre estate into a dairy farm, said Gladys Berry, vice presi-

Bellevue farms before WWII

Much of what is today central Bellevue used to be covered with berry, vegetable and dairy farms. Here are some of them:

1. J. Tremper Holly Farm
2. J. Potier Argyll Fruit Farm
3. F. Boddy Dairy/T. Yabuke Greenhouses
4. Mink Ranch
5. Gilmore Bros. Fox Farms
6. A. Hennig Vineyard
7. C. Gordon Farm
8. F. Delkin Bulb Farm
9. G. Edwards Lily Garden
10. P. Downey Homestead
11. Cruse-Hill Farm/Brunton Horse Farm
12. T. Numoto Farm
13. Rose Chicken Farm/ Sydnor Blueberry Farm
14. T. Hirotaka Farm
15. Campbell/Stetson/Hamley Fruit and Vegetable Farm
16. Y. Sakaguchi Farm
17. R.T. Reid LaBelle Farms
18. J. Kelfner Vineyards
19. F. Winters Farm
20. A. Balatico Fruit and Vegetable Farm
21. Multiple-family farms: W. Hirai, K. Yamagiwa, R. Fuwa, T. Hayashida, H. Aramaki, T. Suguro, H. Takeshita, M. Hashiguchi, and E. Mashiyama
22. Bellevue's Grower's Association Packing and Shipping Warehouse
23. Morelli Bros. Chicken Farm
24. Carlsen Chicken Farm
25. Early Marymoor Dairy Farm
26. Peterson Hill multiple-family farms: T. Yoshin, E. Tamaye, Y. Yamaguchi, G. Nomura, D. Tamate, K. Shimogaki, T. Kamihara, M. Yamaguchi
27. Wm. Duey Twin Valley Dairy
28. Tony Aries Farm
29. Ove Larsen Homestead /Blueberry Farm
30. Chris Nelson Phantom Lake Dairy
31. Hayes Turkey Farm
32. E. Shiraishi Farm

dent of the Woodinville Historical Society.

"It was an immaculate farm," Berry said. "The milkers all wore white, and everything was clean, clean."

The Pickering Barn in Issaquah, now surrounded by a shopping center and offices, was the centerpiece

Grazing land has been partly supplanted by freeways as the Eastside's farmland disappears.

THE SEATTLE TIMES, 1979

of the largest dairy farm in the city around the turn of the century. Darigold, still churning out butter and other products today, built its venerable creamery nearby in 1909.

In the Snoqualmie River Valley north of Duvall, a historic farm district known as Dutchman's Row still is home to dairy-farming families, the last vestiges of the farming community that thrived here beginning in the 1880s. The Row today is officially known as West Snoqualmie River Road Northeast.

The district's nickname was coined in the 1940s in honor of the predominantly Dutch homesteaders who settled there in the 1910s and '20s, lured in part by the success of Carnation Farm.

The 1,550-acre dairy farm, the area's largest employer, was so important that residents of the town of Tolt changed the city's name to Carnation in its honor.

The farm was purchased in 1916 by E.A. Stuart, founder of the Carnation Co. He converted the farm into a state-of-the-art research center and dairy-cow breeding facility. Cows raised at the farm often yielded record-breaking amounts of milk, and they enjoyed near-celebrity status.

End of an era

Residential development, escalating property values and rising livestock-feed prices killed off many of the farms in the Sammamish and Snoqualmie valleys.

King County has attempted to stall the gradual disappearance of farming on the Eastside. It has acquired the development rights to more than 780 acres of farmland and restricted it to agricultural use. Still, many of the larger lots go unused.

Small specialty farmers represent the future of Eastside farming if there is to be a future at all, experts say. But some, including Stringfellow, remain defiant.

In 1969, a year after his father sold the family farm, Stringfellow started his own beef-cattle ranch and Christmas-tree farm — Middle Fork S Ranch — a half-mile east of North Bend. The 100-acre farm is one of the last operating farm in the Upper Snoqualmie River Valley, he said.

But in 2002, Stringfellow was torn between staying on a farm he said is "in my blood" and leaving because of a 258-unit apartment complex approved to be built a few yards from his property line.

NOTABLE EARLY FARMS AND FARMERS

• The **Zante** family, immigrants from the Philippines, started a 17-acre vegetable farm south of downtown Woodinville in 1920. King County has been negotiating to buy the farm to preserve it.

• In 1912, the **Morelli** family from Italy raised chickens on 60 acres near 148th Avenue Northeast and Northeast 51st Street in Redmond. Today, Microsoft's west campus occu-

pies much of the former homestead, and the rest is occupied by big new homes. Some members of the family still live on a tiny patch of the original farm.

• A half-dozen Italian families, including the **Zanassis** and **Pignataros,** shared land south of the **Zante** farm in the Sammamish River Valley. The families hauled vegetables by truck to Seattle markets. From 1922 to 1970,

theirs was the largest "truck farm" in the area.

• **Edward B. Tremper** started raising "fine English holly" on Yarrow Point in 1902, using 1,000 shoots he imported from Europe. In 1929 the journal Nature proclaimed Tremper's the largest holly ranch in the nation. Tremper's farm had expanded to 3,000 acres by 1940.

CHAPTER 33

HISTORY ON THE FLY

For decades airports dotted the Eastside to support a high interest in aviation

At one time, pilots had a choice of Eastside airports. They could land small planes at two Bellevue airports, at Issaquah or Renton, or on Finn Hill. Seaplanes were welcome at bases in Kirkland, Renton and Kenmore.

Businessmen dreamed of even mightier wings for the Eastside: Bellevue once was the preferred site for a regional airport.

That was 50 years ago, when land was cheap.

Like logging, railroading, mining and farming, the heyday of Eastside aviation gave way to housing tracts and automobiles.

But from the 1940s to 1980, several Eastside airports were active as interest in aviation soared around the region. After their World War II service, former Army Air Forces pilots switched to small airplanes, and veterans from other military branches cashed in their GI Bill educational benefits at flight schools.

Entrepreneurs capitalized on the passion by developing airstrips and offering lessons.

"We pilots tried all of them," said octogenarian Marvin Michael of Bellevue. "You'd go from one airport to another."

As the Eastside developed, land became an increasingly valuable commodity. Taxes rose. Neighborhoods changed. Noise became an issue. And developers greedily eyed the acres of runways and taxiways.

One by one, big X's were painted at the end of the runways — a signal to pilots that the runways are

NANCY DUNNAM

closed. Now, most small general aviation fields on the Eastside are notations in pilots' logbooks.

Only two remain active today: Kenmore Air Harbor and Renton Airport.

Bellevue Airfield: Arthur A. Nordhoff founded the Bellevue Airfield in 1941, but because of the war it wouldn't get off the ground until 1945. Nordhoff had been an Army aviator during World War I; his daughter, Nancy Dunnam, flew in the Women's Air Service Pilots during World War II.

A family operation, the 160-acre strip was north of

Bellevue Airfield, shown in 1969, was north of Interstate 90 (foreground) and east of 156th Avenue Northeast. It closed in 1983.

BY SHERRY GRINDELAND

today's Interstate 90 and east of 156th Avenue Southeast. Neighbors included a gun club, a turkey ranch, a mink farm and the Bellevue-area garbage dump at the north end of the field.

By the early 1970s, the airfield averaged 51,000 take-offs and landings a year.

"We never had a control tower, but we had runway lights that operated until 11 at night," recalled Arthur E. Nordhoff, son of the founder. Business often picked up during winter months when fog socked in Renton and Boeing fields, he said.

"Once when The Beatles were coming to town, teenagers heard a rumor they weren't going to land at Sea-Tac or Boeing," Nordhoff said. "So for an afternoon we had a bunch of giggling teenagers around. Of course, The Beatles didn't come to Bellevue."

Hit hard by escalating real-estate and other taxes, the airport closed May 2, 1983.

Mercer Inlet Airfield: When her airport opened in July 1946, Lolita Havercamp told a newspaper reporter that she was the only great-grandmother in the country who owned a landing field. Her family owned the land at the mouth of Coal Creek for 58 years before Havercamp developed the 2,050-foot-long gravel runway.

By 1948 it was called Lake Air Park. Today the same area houses the upscale Newport Shores development.

Issaquah Skyport: Airplanes hadn't been invented when William Pickering, governor of Washington Territory in the 1860s, homesteaded the area between I-90 and Lake Sammamish. His was the first dairy farm in Issaquah — and the last.

A century later the Issaquah Skyport occupied 30 acres of the original homestead and catered to sky-divers and soaring planes, both carried to launching altitudes by small aircraft.

In a 1980 interview, Linn Emrich said that when he began operating the airport in 1961, he saw more herons, seagulls, deer, hawks and pigeons than cars and people.

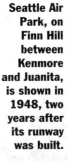

The North Seattle Air Park, on Finn Hill between Kenmore and Juanita, is shown in 1948, two years after its runway was built.

This Eastside site in Bellevue was a candidate for a major airport in the 1940s. But the Bow Lake site was picked because it was halfway between Seattle and Tacoma.

Old Eastside airports

1 Kenmore Air Harbor *(still exists)*
2 North Seattle Air Park *(gone)*
3 Kirkland Seaplane Terminal *(gone)*
4 Bellevue Airfield *(gone)*
5 Mercer Inlet Airfield *(gone)*
6 Renton Airport and Will Rogers-Wiley Post Memorial Seaplane Base *(still exists)*
7 Issaquah Skyport *(gone)*
8 Duvall *(gone)*

THE SEATTLE TIMES

The airport closed in July 1987.

Today, parking lots for Pickering Place stores cover the flat, grassy area that cushioned landing sky-divers.

North Seattle Air Park: In 1946 Maurice Proctor and A.J. Menard used a World War II surplus bulldozer to clear a 2,600-foot runway on Finn Hill between Kenmore and Juanita.

The 86-acre airport grew, providing four hangars and space for 60 to 70 planes.

In a 1989 newspaper article, Proctor recalled flying over the Eastside and Seattle with a loudspeaker system, playing Christmas carols and commercials for area businesses.

The airport was sold in 1952 and closed soon after. Today, Inglewood Shopping Center and houses in Inglewood Hills cover the old runways and taxiways.

Kirkland Seaplane Terminal: Although float-planes can easily land on Lake Washington near Kirkland, according to aviation maps there once was a seaplane terminal near downtown. It's probably a boat pier today, although local pilots don't recall its exact location.

Kenmore: Bob Munro opened his seaplane base at the north end of Lake Washington in 1946. Unlike other postwar shoestring aviation operations, Kenmore Air Harbor thrived and still serves the seaplane community.

His flying service ferries people, boat parts and food to remote locations.

Duvall: The small private strip once owned by Cal Evans has been filled with small houses and mobile homes.

What was notable, according to Seattle Times reporter Ron Judd, who grew up in Duvall, was the offer Evans made several decades ago.

He planned a high-end community, with a couple dozen homes spread among wooded lots and connected to the runway by taxiways. (A similar development, Crest Airpark, exists today near Kent.)

Although the City Council approved the project, and the developer argued it would save the land from subdivision, residents complained, and the project never happened. Today the development has eight times as many houses as the original proposal — and no airstrip.

Renton: The longest operating Eastside airport was the base for Northwest Air Service as early as 1920, when the company won a mail-route contract between Seattle and Victoria, B.C. At that time the airport was called Bryn Mawr Field. In 1928 it was renamed the Renton Airport, although for many years it went by both names.

At the southwestern tip of Lake Washington, the airfield served land and seaplanes. By 1928, Northwest Air Service had become the primary Northwest facility for changing a plane's floats to wheels and vice versa.

That's why the seaplane portion today is called the Will Rogers-Wiley Post Memorial Field. Rogers was a beloved American humorist and entertainer of the 1920s and '30s, and Post was an adventurer, famed for his solo round-the-world flight.

In 1935, the two friends embarked on a round-the-world flight, landing their Lockheed Orion Explorer at Renton. The wheels were exchanged for floats, against the advice of Lockheed engineers.

Rogers and Post departed Renton on Aug. 7. A few days later they were killed 12 miles southeast of Barrow, Alaska, when the plane developed engine trouble and did a backward nosedive on departure.

In 1935, Will Rogers, left, and Wiley Post embarked on a round-the-world flight, landing their Lockheed Orion Explorer at the Renton Airport.

SEATTLE TIMES ARCHIVES

As part of the World War II effort, the U.S. government rebuilt the Renton Airport to accommodate large planes in 1942. It was expanded again in 1944, built up on 450,000 yards of dirt dredged from the bottom of Lake Washington.

Lake Sammamish Airport: Also called the Seattle Midlakes Airport, it would have changed the entire development of the Eastside, bringing jets instead of cars, businesses instead of residential tracts.

It was never built.

In the late 1930s, Seattle's Boeing Field was crowded. If aviation and the area were to grow, another regional airfield was needed. Civic leaders studied Jefferson Park in Seattle, Mercer Island, a Lake Sammamish site (between today's Lake Hills and Spiritwood neighborhoods), and an area near Bow Lake.

The 100-acre Lake Sammamish site was the first choice, Bow Lake the runner-up.

Tacoma civic leaders stepped in and offered $100,000 toward the development of the Bow Lake site. The Navy also preferred it, because, when combined with Sand Point Naval Station and Boeing Field, Bow Lake provided a three-point defense base for the Seattle area.

The choice delighted United Airlines leaders because it cornered both the Seattle and Tacoma market.

Today the Bow Lake site is known as Seattle-Tacoma International Airport.

CHAPTER 34

RENTON

Once a factory town, the 'Gateway to the East' now looks to diversification

RENTON HISTORICAL SOCIETY, 1912

For more than 100 years, Renton has been a big wheel in manufacturing circles. Renton factories produced trains, planes, wagons, trucks, tanks, bottles, macaroni, ice, twine, coal briquettes, lumber and shingles. It was home to the world's largest paving-brick factory in the early 1900s.

An early cabin on the Christian Clymer homestead.

The town that straddles the southeastern shore of Lake Washington has sported nicknames that matched its blue-collar roots — The Brick Capital of the World, the Town of Payrolls and the Birthplace of Modern Commercial Aviation.

But it all began with coal.

Henry Tobin discovered coal in the Renton hills in 1853. That was the same year Adelaide Andrews opened the first school in King County on the Christian Clymer homestead just west of today's Renton Airport.

Tobin and four other men

founded the Duwamish Coal Co. but never found financing to begin mining. Instead, Tobin built a sawmill on the Black River in 1854 and with his wife, Diana, staked a claim to 320 acres in what is today's downtown Renton. He died about a year later.

The land that Tobin helped settle had for centuries been a hub for Native American tribes. Duwamish longhouses once stood on Earlington Golf Course and Renton High School grounds. The area was lush with wildlife.

The Black River, which flowed out of Lake Washington near the airport, was joined by the Cedar, and both rivers flowed into the Duwamish. Tribes from as far north as Alaska arrived in 40-foot canoes to trade near today's Maplewood Golf Course.

Early settlers used the same route for tug boats

The Renton Coal Co., which was started in 1873, operated a mine built into the hillside, east of what is now Interstate 405.

Diana Tobin Smithers

BY SHERRY GRINDELAND

and paddle wheelers, coming from Seattle through the Duwamish River, the Black River, then into Lake Washington, the Sammamish River and Lake Sammamish to trade as far inland as Issaquah.

The rivers deposited rich delta soil in the Renton lowlands, and when Tobin's widow married Erasmus Smithers in 1857, their dairy farm prospered. Yet it was the coal under the hills that provided Renton the impetus to become a town.

William Renton, who made his fortune in timber mills around the Puget Sound area, financed the Renton Coal Co. in 1873. The city was platted two years later and named in his honor.

Capt. William Renton

Coal used locally

Coal would be king for more than 50 years. Mine tunnels stretched from today's Interstate 405 almost to Kent.

Unlike nearby mining operations such as Newcastle and Issaquah that shipped coal to other markets, Renton's coal primarily was used in local manufacturing. It fired the Renton Clay Works, for example, which produced building bricks, road pavers and clay pipes for water lines and sewers.

Another big customer was the Pacific Car and Foundry, which opened in 1907, then burned to the ground, was rebuilt and went on to produce wagons, rail cars and trucks.

The blue-collar workers, a mix of immigrant cultures mostly from Europe, had a reputation for playing hard. At one point in the late 1800s, there were 875 citizens and 18 saloons. It was common for miners to carry buckets of beer underground as part of their lunch.

RENTON HISTORICAL SOCIETY, 1914

The Denny Renton Clay and Coal Co. was located across from what is now Carco Theater.

Dr. Adolph Bronson built a 15-room hospital in 1911 at the southeast corner of Second and Main streets.

RENTON HISTORICAL SOCIETY

RENTON HISTORICAL SOCIETY

Sherman tanks were built at Pacific Car and Foundry during World War II and tested on Cemetery Hill.

But they were also civic-minded. The Renton Miners Association organized the first library in 1903.

Renton had the first hospital on the Eastside. Dr. Adolph Bronson built a 15-room hospital in 1911 and for decades, seriously injured miners, loggers, sawmill workers and farmers on the Eastside were transported to Renton for medical care.

That same year the city nearly washed away. At 8:30 a.m. on Sunday, Nov. 11, church bells rang out — not calling people to worship but to alert townspeople to a flood. No lives were lost, but the entire flatland of downtown Renton was inundated by the overflowing Cedar and Black rivers.

It was weeks before the town dried out.

Gateway to the East

When the Montlake Cut opened in 1916, the lowering of Lake Washington eliminated the Black River. Draining swamp land eventually was filled and became home to Boeing.

Although that ended the paddle-wheeler and tugboat traffic, Renton still called itself the "Gateway to the East."

Until the opening of the first floating bridge across Lake Washington in 1940, the name was accurate. Most automobile and truck traffic coming from Seattle to the Eastside and the Cascades went through Renton.

The Seattle Walla Walla Railroad reached Renton in 1887, and by 1904 the Lake Washington Beltline connected Renton, Bellevue, Kirkland and Woodinville.

Sunset Highway, the first automobile route that connected Seattle to Spokane and points east, ran through Renton.

As car traffic grew and asphalt became the road material of choice, Renton's brick trade waned. Electrical power surged in popularity, and the demand for coal subsided. As the Depression hit, the last Renton coal mines shut down.

But it wasn't long before the city rebounded in a new direction. Less than a mile from the mine

RENTON HISTORICAL SOCIETY

entrances, Puget Sound Traction, Light and Power Co. began construction of the Shuffleton Power Plant near today's Gene Coulon Memorial Beach Park.

The steam turbines, powered by waste wood fiber from sawmills called "hog fuel," provided the electricity that replaced coal in homes and factories. One section of the plant was running by 1929 but, because of the Depression, Puget Power never built the entire complex. The plant was torn down in 2001.

11,000 fans attended the opening of Longacres Race Track in 1933.

Racing to Renton

Renton became a Mecca for horse-race fans in 1933 when then-Gov. Clarence Martin legalized horse-race betting on March 3. More than 3,000 workers toiled nearly around the clock for 28 days to build Longacres Race Track. The first race was held Aug. 3, 1933, when 11,000 people watched On Rush win the Inaugural Handicap.

The track was dark two summers during World

Boeing, located at the southern tip of Lake Washington, built about 1,000 B-29s by the end of WWII.

War II. An anti-aircraft gun was set up midfield. The land eventually was sold to Boeing, and the last race was held Sept. 21, 1992.

By 1940, The Boeing Airplane Co. had decided on Renton as the site for a large plant to build seaplanes. As WWII wound up, it switched to B-29 bombers.

The small Bryn Mawr Airport was rebuilt to accommodate the heavier traffic — round-the-clock shifts pushed 1,000 planes out the door to the runway by the end of the war.

The nearby Pacific Car and Foundry, which had built trucks and thousands of boxcars for railroads around the world, began building Sherman tanks.

The influx of workers meant schools went to triple shifts.

Driving at night during the wartime blackout became challenging. Tanks clanked through city streets out to today's Maplewood Golf Course, where they were run up and down Cemetery Hill for field tests. (Cemetery Hill became famous in 1970, when rock star Jimi Hendrix was buried in Greenwood Memorial Park.)

After the war, the city's economy slowed down. Pacific Car and Foundry — which became Paccar in the 1970s — switched back to trucks and rail cars (rail-car production ceased in the early 1980s).

Boeing was harder hit in the post-war years. It closed its Renton plant and went through massive lay-offs. The plant reopened in 1948 and in 1954 started producing 707 jets for commercial use.

By 1966, the company employed 38,600 workers at its Renton plant. By 1995, its operations in the city covered 7.7 million square feet.

However, the company that has weathered numerous economic ups and downs during its 80-year history announced in 2002 that it would vacate 2 million square feet of space as it struggled with the impact of a national recession.

The loss reinforced Renton's push to diversify its economic base, which now includes such companies as Valley Medical Center, IKEA, Wizards of the Coast and Classmates.com.

For the 21st century, the city has adopted a new slogan — "Ahead of the Curve" — and is focusing on revitalizing its downtown.

Potential developments, such as an office complex at the Port Quendell sawmill site, could ensure that Renton will continue to stay ahead of any future economic curves.

After WWII, Boeing turned out the KC-135 Stratotanker planes.

Sources include Renton Historical Society & Museum Quarterly, "Renton from Coal to Jets" by Morda C. Slauson, "Renton: Where the Water Took Wing," by David M. Buerge

CHAPTER 35

DEFENDING THE EASTSIDE

World War II volunteers and Cold War missile sites played key military roles

Today's peaceful valleys and hilltops yield few remnants of the muscle and missiles that once made the Eastside a strategic defense site.

Forts were built along the Snoqualmie River to fend off Native American attacks. During World War II volunteers looked for enemy aircraft from watchtowers in Clyde Hill and Woodinville. In the 1950s troops kept missiles poised for launch in Redmond and Issaquah as Cold War tensions mounted.

In 1855 Native Americans came through Snoqualmie or Yakima pass and attacked the small town of Seattle.

Soldiers from the Northern Battalion were sent up the Snoqualmie River. They followed an Indian trail, building a string of forts along the way: Patterson, Tilton, Alden and Smalley. According to one historian, the forts were named after the officers in the expedition.

Dubbing these hastily constructed outposts "forts" was a generous description. Old drawings of three — Forts Tilton, Alden and Smalley — show log buildings, not the traditional high walls associated with forts of the Old West. Fort Tilton reportedly measured 14 by 16 feet.

Fort Patterson was near Fall City. Fort Tilton was just below Tokul Creek where it runs into the Snoqualmie River.

Some historians think there may have been one more fort or stockade near Cedar Falls.

The local Indians, the Snoqualmies, were cordial to white settlers, so the stockades and forts were deserted when the threat from the Eastern tribes dissipated. Within two years, Jerimiah Borst, an early settler in the North Bend-Meadowbrook area, converted Fort

Eastside defense sites

Legend:
- Old forts
- WWII watchtowers
- Missile sites

Map labels: Puget Sound, Seattle, Woodinville, Snoqualmie River, SNOHOMISH COUNTY / KING COUNTY, Duvall, Tolt River, Redmond, Clyde Hill, Bellevue, Lake Washington, Carnation, North Fork, Fort Patterson, Lake Sammamish, Issaquah, Fall City, Fort Tilton, Snoqualmie, Fort Alden, Cougar Mountain, Renton, Fort Smalley, North Bend, Green River, Cedar River, South Fork, Denny Creek

0 — 10 Miles

THE SEATTLE TIMES

Alden into his home. The other stockades were also adopted by settlers.

The home front was quiet during the next few wars — largely bypassed by the Civil and Spanish-American wars and World War I. World War II was another story.

BY SHERRY GRINDELAND

THE SEATTLE TIMES, 1942

This 30-foot watchtower was built in the Redmond area. The shelter in this 1942 photo has windows on all sides and in the roof to track aircraft.

Vulnerable to attack

After the Dec. 7, 1941, attack on Pearl Harbor, Eastside residents mobilized like other Americans.

The West Coast was considered vulnerable to a Japanese invasion. The Lake Washington Shipyards in Kirkland and Boeing were major targets.

The shipyards geared up to help rebuild the Navy. Naval pilots were trained at Sand Point on the lake's west shore.

People were scared. They worried about bombs from an air attack and about Japanese soldiers parachuting into the area.

An anti-aircraft battery moved onto Cougar Mountain in Issaquah. Two were set up on Mercer Island. Hilltop observation posts or watchtowers were rapidly constructed in several Eastside communities, including Redmond, Clyde Hill, Woodinville and Duvall.

As men marched off to war, women, retirees and high-school students volunteered for round-the-clock duty at the posts, dubbed OPs.

"My grandparents played a special deck of cards, marked on the back with different kinds of airplanes," said Lee Maxwell of Bellevue. "They lived in Duvall and volunteered for tower duty there. The cards helped them learn what the different aircraft looked like."

Called the Aircraft Warning Service, watchers on duty telephoned headquarters when airplanes were spotted. Volunteers and military people at headquarters tracked aircraft throughout the Puget Sound area to be certain they were all friendly.

The towers were cold and drafty. Often two people shared duty, one to pace the deck outside while the other warmed up inside. Nearby residents or restaurants donated sandwiches and coffee.

High winds once blew the roof off the Clyde Hill tower.

It was a time of blackout, meaning lights weren't supposed to be visible after dark. But one military unit could light up the skies.

Near today's intersection of Southeast Newport Way and Highway 900 in Issaquah, troops were assigned to maintain spotlights. In case of attack, they would provide the light for the batteries on top of Cougar Mountain.

"They built barracks out of wooden shipping boxes that had been used to ship airplane engines to Boeing," Issaquah historian Eric Erickson said.

People were warned to be on the lookout for sabotage — spies who wanted to slow down the war effort. Japanese families were sent to internment camps.

The proximity to Sand Point meant training flights crisscrossed Kirkland, Bellevue, Redmond and Issaquah. Fighter pilots swooped over Issaquah, learning to handle their planes in the drafts off Tiger Mountain.

Sometime in early summer 1944, a bomber on a training flight crashed on Kirkland's Rose Hill, near what today is the intersection of Interstate 405 and Northeast 85th Street. There were no serious injuries, but military personnel surrounded the site and kept civilians away.

Once the war was over, the towers disappeared and the decks of cards were stuffed in drawers.

Three sections of the double-platoon installation at Redmond were ready for launching Nike Ajax missiles in June 1957.

THE SEATTLE TIMES, 1957

Steel doors cover missile silos at Cougar Mountain in 1976.

THE SEATTLE TIMES, 1976

Eastside mobilizes again

When the Cold War froze relations between the Soviet Union and the United States, the Eastside again mobilized.

In the 1950s missile bases were built behind massive fences in Issaquah, Redmond and the Bothell area. Other Puget Sound communities housed similar bases.

The U.S. prepared for the worst-case scenario — an atomic attack. Air defense around the country called for Nike missile stations near prime targets, including 11 in the Seattle area.

By 1957 the Eastside sites were fully armed and fully staffed. Guard dogs and handlers walked the fence perimeters at the 23-acre Nike control center on Redmond's Education Hill. A 27-acre launch site was at nearby Novelty Hill.

The military presence was well known. Army soldiers in Redmond, for example, drove a flatbed truck showing off a Nike missile in the annual Derby Days parade. But the missiles, made obsolete by longer-range weapons based elsewhere, were removed within a decade.

Redmond High School was built on part of the old Education Hill missile site. The Federal Emergency Management Agency's regional office is headquartered in the old Bothell-area missile site.

The Issaquah Nike missile site and the former World War II anti-aircraft battery land is now part of Cougar Mountain Regional Park.

THE SEATTLE TIMES, 1957

Calibrating a search radar at the Redmond Nike site in June 1957 were, from left, Lt. Clayton Hunt, specialists Dean Thorndike, Franz Kirstein and Edward Kunst.

Sources include "A History of the Snoqualmie Valley" by Ada Snyder Hill, "Snoqualmie Pass, From Indian Trail to Interstate" by Yvonne Prater and "Our Town Redmond" by Nancy Way.

CHAPTER 36

BELLEVUE

The early planners' vision: Bellevue would be everything Seattle wasn't

Bellevue was still a town of fields, forests and gravel roads when it incorporated in 1953. It was also a city vibrating with a sense of destiny.

Here a small group of men — and one in particular — believed they could create the city of the future, a model of "gracious" homes and bustling commerce that would polish the suburban dream to brilliance.

That it had a population just shy of 6,000 did nothing to betray an enthusiasm for growth and the future that bordered on audacious.

THE SEATTLE TIMES, 1948

Seattle was king, but on the east side of Lake Washington, people promised better parks, stronger schools, cleaner industry, a modern downtown and "a city with space for spreading out your house and yard, space to live and space to play."

In the two decades that followed cityhood, Bellevue became something of a self-fulfilled prophecy. But not, as many had hoped, a panacea for the urban ills that drove the post-World War II generation from the cities.

During those early years, few other cities embraced the promise of suburbia with Bellevue's vigor.

That vision may seem naive, even fantastic now. But at the time Bellevue was ringed by enough land to inspire developers and convince officials they really could create a better city.

The land had always been there, but it was other factors that lifted Bellevue out of the backwaters of the Mercer Slough and set it on course to become the hub of the Eastside.

Bridge changes everything

Before the first floating bridge opened in 1940, Bellevue was famous for its annual Strawberry Festival and little else. Settled by a handful of pioneers in the late 1800s, it grew slowly into a community huddled around a few shops on Main Street.

The bridge, however, changed everything. The long trip around the lake was now a 20-minute dash across it. When the tolls were lifted in 1949, there was nothing between a generation of families — the parents of the baby boom — and their new homes in the suburbs.

By the early 1950s, the mushrooming population already strained the sewer and water systems. A study for the school district predicted 100,000 people would eventually settle in Bellevue, a realization that shocked the community into action.

Worried that King County oversight wasn't enough to manage the boom, Bellevue incorporated in 1953, with $500 in credit from a local bank and a rented "city hall" on the second floor of the Veterans of Foreign Wars hall.

Downtown Bellevue in the years after World War II was a planner's dream and a developer's gold mine. Above, 104th Street Northeast (Bellevue Way Northeast) runs past Bellevue Square, middle right.

BY J. MARTIN McOMBER

There was little more to downtown Bellevue in 1948 than the collection of shops and restaurants on Main Street, but the community was feeling the pressure to grow.

Outlining a city

It is a testament to just how concerned Bellevue was about growth that the City Council's first act was to create a Planning Commission, not a Police Department, to bring order and form to the new city.

One of the first commissioners was the late Fred Herman, a young architect whose enthusiasm for the task of creating a city — an instant city some called it — led to his appointment as Bellevue's first planning director.

"(It) was darn near a clean slate to start with," he said in a 1990 interview. "There were a few things around, but nothing really in the way in terms of looking forward to the city we envisioned happening."

That city, the commission agreed, would be neat, orderly, efficient, spacious, everything older U.S. cities weren't. Neighborhoods would be separated from commercial and industrial areas. The downtown would be built for automobiles, not the pedestrians and streetcars that shaped other cities.

"They would almost stop at nothing if they thought it would produce something superior to what they knew when they lived in Cleveland, or wherever the heck they came from, because most people came from someplace (else)," he said.

In his cramped office, Herman unrolled sheets of plastic over a map of Bellevue. He drew the different zones, streets, parks and schools that didn't exist.

When the sheets were laid on top of each other, the outlines of the new city emerged for the first time.

By 1954, the city had passed a comprehensive development plan that received national attention. Two years after incorporation, voters had approved a $1.3 million bond measure to build new schools and $1 million more for a new water system.

In early 1956, Bellevue was named one of 11 "All America" cities by Look magazine because of the way it was dealing with a growth rate that had nearly doubled the population in three years.

Growth became a selling point for Bellevue, which began to market the good suburban life under the slogan "over the bridge to gracious living."

A 92-page book pitching Bellevue and its businesses breathlessly proclaimed:

"A new and different kind of city, Bellevue — built the way its people wanted it to be. And building yet,

★ ★ ★
ALL-AMERICA
CITY
BELLEVUE
WASHINGTON

Rhil Reilly celebrates 1953 incorporation with an impromptu sign revision.

growing yet, with much expansion yet to come. . . . No more jammed-together apartment buildings full of cubicles, the cramped together houses, the look-alikes without space to live and breathe and roam. No more the houses without yards."

Catering to the car

While massive subdivisions began to spread, Herman and others focused on creating the new downtown.

Even before the city was incorporated, businesses were already being designed to cater to the car. In 1946, Kemper Freeman, son of a wealthy publishing family, began building one of the nation's first planned suburban shopping centers, Bellevue Square.

Herman and others saw the potential of the automobile to change the nature of downtown. They laid out huge blocks, "superblocks" as they called them, along a grid of four- and six-lane streets.

"We had lots of cars, not an awful lot of them, but quite a few cars," he recalled.

"And so we looked at the speed of a car as opposed to the speed of a pedestrian, things like that, and the dollar value of land, which at that time was relatively cheap in terms of its use.

"So we said, 'Maybe we should try to design blocks that fit the car.'"

They did. Buildings were set back from the road and landscaped to give the downtown an open feel. Businesses were required to provide parking because the streets were for moving cars, not storing them.

Fred Herman

One of the first major projects was rebuilding Northeast 104th Street (now Bellevue Way Northeast) and transforming a two-lane road with open gutters into a gateway for the city.

"Immediately, it completely changed the look of Bellevue, it gave a different impression because here was a six-lane street in the middle of no place, almost," Herman said. "All the rest of the streets were oiled,

dirt or gravel. . . . But that made such an impression, that the concept of continuing to develop this city became accepted."

Not just a suburb

By 1956 the city had wooed Puget Power to move its headquarters from Seattle to Bellevue, leading Freeman to announce prophetically, but prematurely, "We're no longer a bedroom community for Seattle; we are a job center."

Over the next decade, Bellevue filled in much the way Herman had envisioned. Fifteen years after incorporation, the city had grown to nearly 30,000. In another five years, it more than doubled to 63,000.

By the early 1970s, Herman and his Planning Commission were peering still further in the future, building a model that showed a downtown of double-decked streets that would whisk cars to self-contained blocks of high-rises.

By then, much of Bellevue had been filled in.

While the perception of the city as a bedroom community lingered, Bellevue had become one of the state's largest cities. Its days as the ideal suburb would soon be gone.

A late 1950s brochure promises growth and "gracious living."

CHAPTER 37

CHANGING CHANNELS

Decades of dredging turned the winding Sammamish River into a straight ditch

Equipment in the foreground is used to dredge the Sammamish River to reclaim the lowland near Bothell.

ARMY CORPS OF ENGINEERS, 1964

Stand along much of the Sammamish River, perhaps at Northeast 116th Street, and the scene appears almost blissfully placid. The 60 Acres soccer fields are there. Bike riders speed past on a riverfront trail. Rockets and model airplanes soar at a park.

Forty years ago, those things were impossible. The area was routinely submerged, flooded by the river.

Many of Redmond's newest buildings, including City Hall, the Rivertrail Townhomes and new shopping centers, all stand where brush and cattails grew.

The development was possible because of public-works projects that once were virtually unquestioned yet probably would be unthinkable today.

The work that changed the valley stretched over more than 50 years and wasn't finished until the 1960s.

It turned a meandering 30-mile river into essentially a slow-flowing ditch, its surface often 20 feet below the level of the surrounding terrain.

The dredging and straightening of the Sammamish River also had a dramatic effect on what was one of the richest wetlands in the Puget Sound region. It also had major, if unintended, effects on the salmon that once filled the river.

BY PEYTON WHITELY

OLD SEATTLE PAPERWORKS

A couple enjoy a picnic around the turn of the 20th century along the Sammamish Slough. In the distance is the original railroad trestle. This photograph was taken at what is now a park near Wayne Golf Course.

The Sammamish River contained about half the salmon and trout populations spawning in the Lake Washington watershed, according to a 1950 state report. Redmond's original name, in fact, was Salmonberg because it had so many fish.

Today extensive efforts are being made to restore the salmon runs, but changing the once-meandering river into a straight channel with little shade and bordered by acres of parking have made that a substantial challenge.

In 1895, river was a swamp

A century ago, the present appearance of the Sammamish River would have been inconceivable.

An 1895 survey map shows the river winding through swamp land. Several now-forgotten towns with names such as Derby and York dotted the valley.

For about 20 years in the late 1800s, the river was the main route to much of the Eastside.

Although the distance from the river's source in Lake Sammamish to Kenmore where it empties into Lake Washington is now about 10 miles, traveling the river then was a 30-mile trip, usually made by barges pushed by crews using poles.

A major navigational advance occurred in 1884, when a 42-foot scow named the Squak, built at shipyards in Houghton and powered by a 12-horsepower steam engine, began running the river. Such river trips soon would disappear.

Tracks for the Seattle, Lake Shore & Eastern Railway were laid to Bothell in 1887 and by 1888 had been brought down the west side of the valley, then to the eastern edge of Lake Sammamish and on to Issaquah.

Boats did remain as the chief way to cross Lake Washington, however, until the Mercer Island Floating Bridge was opened in 1940.

Shipping ran as late as 1916 to Bothell, considered the head of navigation, with such steamers as the Evril, Duck Hunter and May Blossom following the river's curves.

The May Blossom was one of a small fleet of steamers that carried tourists up the river to Bothell before roads.

PUGET SOUND MARITIME HISTORICAL SOCIETY / 1908 OR 1909

THE SEATTLE TIMES, 1958

Old, new river routes

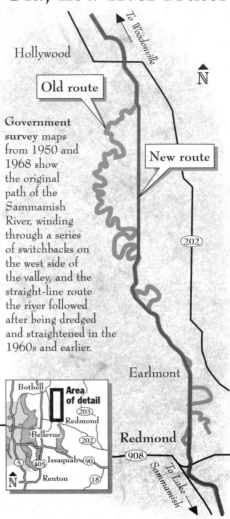

Government survey maps from 1950 and 1968 show the original path of the Sammamish River, winding through a series of switchbacks on the west side of the valley, and the straight-line route the river followed after being dredged and straightened in the 1960s and earlier.

THE SEATTLE TIMES

Outboard speedboats race along the slough in the popular event, begun in 1928, that drew as many as 50,000 spectators. The races ended in 1976.

Commercial navigation on the river finally was ended by still another now-unthinkable project, the construction of the Ballard Locks, providing a route to Puget Sound.

Opening the Locks in 1916 lowered Lake Washington 9 feet and drained much of the Sammamish River. Steamers could no longer make it to Bothell. The river continued to be used for moving logs to mills, leading to countless logjams.

By 1917, James Clise wrote to the Army Corps of Engineers about jams blocking the river, expressing his concern about the detrimental effects on his country estate, Willowmoor. (Today, the 1904 Clise Mansion is the site of the county's Marymoor Museum of Eastside History.)

That same year, the Sammamish River Drainage District was started, and dredging began to improve flows.

Annual flooding remained a part of life in the valley for decades, however. A 1964 newspaper article told how farmers found it impossible to use their land for about half of each year, with as much as 7 feet of water covering much of the valley.

King County dredging efforts to curtail the flooding were only partly successful, and decades of discussion about the river ensued.

Corps records about the river fill more than 160 volumes of correspondence, studies and other materials dating to 1912. Federal flood-control aid was approved in 1948, but it wasn't until 1961 that the money was appropriated.

Dreamy days spent swimming

The river provided for some idyllic times during those years, however, with settlers reminiscing about dreamy days spent at swimming holes before the channel was straightened.

Its original twisty path was the site of "The Sammamish Slough Race" started in 1928. The race drew as many as 50,000 spectators to watch outboard speedboats race the length of the slough, with hydroplanes hitting speeds above 80 mph, crashing into logs, sand bars and the riverbank while observers lined bridges and the shoreline.

The race lost much of its excitement after the final channel straightening in the 1960s, and eventually came to an end after a 1976 accident in which a boat hit a spectator, Ron Clausen. A University of Washington pole vaulter, Clausen suffered a broken leg and never competed again.

In 1963, Dorothy Brant Brazier, a Seattle Times editor, wrote of a trip along the waterway just before

A pipeline dredge is at work along the slough near Bothell.

Seattle Times file, 1964

the straightening project was to begin.

She told of seeing "boys fishing . . . men ploughing, a girl on horseback, dogs racing our boat, cows and horses drinking at the water's edge.

"We slipped past pretty homes, deserted cabins, mills . . . the river winds through rich farmlands and meadows thick with buttercups. There are clumps of cattails and clumps of rushes and floating lily pads."

By July 1963 work on final straightening and dredging had begun under a $3.75 million joint project by the Army Corps of Engineers and King County. When it was completed in 1965, the riverbed had been lowered as much as 7 feet, the tailings placed along the banks and the old channels filled.

The river, "new from source to outlet, will be designed to carry off far greater quantities of floodwater than ever has been recorded during decades of sometimes torrential downpours," project engineer Phillip Bishop said.

Bishop was largely right, although flooding has continued to periodically occur in the area. But other than the reminder of occasional floods, it's hard to visualize what the river and valley must have looked like in 1899, because nothing of it remains today.

Sources include files of The Seattle Times; displays at Marymoor Museum of Eastside History and the Bothell Historical Museum; "Our Town Redmond" by Nancy Way; "The Bothell Interviews, 1975," published by the Northshore School District; "Slough of Memories," compiled by Fred Klein; and "Squak Slough" by Amy Eunice Stickney and Lucile McDonald.

CHAPTER 38

INTERSTATE 405

The highway dramatically changed transportation on the Eastside

MIKE LEVY / THE SEATTLE TIMES, 198?

The biggest man-made object on the Eastside was just a line on a map 50 years ago. At more than 30 miles long and made of millions of tons of concrete and asphalt, Interstate 405 dwarfs any other feature along the eastern edge of Lake Washington.

Transportation was, and perhaps still is, the determining factor in how the Eastside developed, and I-405's impact was instrumental. The roadway radically changed life east of the lake, much like the Lake Washington Floating Bridge did after its completion in 1940.

When I-405 was conceived, much of the area east of Lake Washington was a rural farming area, where Kirkland was the biggest city. The coming of a new highway could scarcely have been of more interest.

A story in the Kirkland weekly newspaper reported that the road would destroy some 50 homes in the city, including such historic residences as the John A. Andreen home built in 1899.

"Inside the home are many pieces of furniture over 100 years old and are still being used by Ellen

Work on HOV lanes began in 1983 and was completed in 2002, with 33 continuous miles stretching from Lynnwood to Tukwila.

BY PEYTON WHITELY

The Interstate 405/Highway 520 interchange had to be rebuilt and a new flyover ramp leading traffic from 520 onto northbound 405 opened in 1993.

Interstate 405

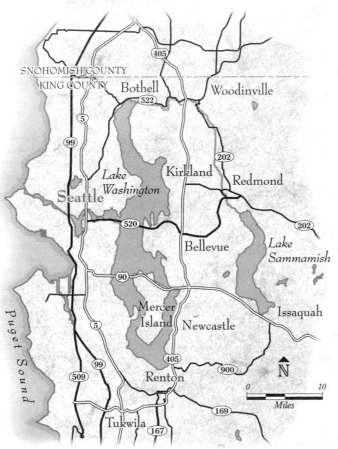

Andreen, who was born here on Rose Hill in 1893," it stated. "She still cooks on a woodstove... the land where Lake Washington High School now stands was once part of their homestead and for years she hiked on the many trails of this area before there were roads."

For Seattle's benefit

It was March 8, 1948, when the Washington state director of highways ordered a new roadway built on the Eastside to provide a speedy bypass around congested Seattle traffic.

It took until 1952 to get the plan approved and purchase access rights. A two-lane roadway was built along part of the route, with plans to someday expand it to four lanes.

But in 1956, President Eisenhower approved what was officially called the Federal-Aid Highway Act of 1956, directing that a national defense and interstate-highway system should be developed — and the future route of I-405 was included.

The resulting interstate system stretches 46,380 miles and took 40 years to build — the biggest public-works project in history.

By November the first part of the new Eastside road — known as Highway 2-A — was done, leading to amazed observations by longtime residents that it was now possible to drive from Kirkland to Bellevue in only four minutes.

But by 1960, Wes Bogart, state highway administrator, was already predicting that the roadway would "someday" have to be made six lanes wide. Just four years later, another highway official said the widening would have to take place within three to four years,

TERESA TAMURA / THE SEATTLE TIMES, 1993

RICHARD S. HEYZA / THE SEATTLE TIMES, 1989

BRUCE McKIM / THE SEATTLE TIMES, 1971

Above, part of the reconfiguring of the S-curves on Interstate 405 in Renton involved tearing down 22 houses, including the one pictured here.

In 1960 Interstate 405 carried 5,300 vehicles a day; a little over 10 years later, increasing volume caused the road to be widened as shown in this stretch just east of Kirkland.

A worker guides a steel girder into place on a new ramp connnecting Interstate 405 South to the Highway 520 East interchange.

because "traffic has increased at a terrific rate."

Alternate routes

The new roadway's effects on the Eastside could have been much different. An alternate route was under consideration as late as 1961.

On Aug. 1, 1961, citizens crowded into the auditorium of W. A. Anderson Junior High School in Bothell to learn about four possible routes for the new highway.

One, known as the "Wayne route," would have passed along the east edge of the Valhalla housing development and the Wayne Golf Course in Bothell, with much discussion centering on a "Wayne Interchange" that would have put a cloverleaf intersection at Bothell Way.

Eventually, a route through the North Creek Valley was picked, between Bothell and Woodinville, leading to multilevel intersections and dense industrial development there, and even a new University of Washington campus. The Wayne Golf Course and Valhalla remain untouched.

By 1963, work was moving rapidly, with connections made at the intersection of what was then called Primary State Highway No. 1, now known as Highway 520.

But it was already clear that the roadway, planned to handle traffic for 20 years, would not be adequate for long. By 1967, the state was scouting for a parallel route for I-405, with a map showing an additional proposed freeway running through Maple Valley, Newcastle and Lake Hills before connecting to Highway 520 at Bridle Trails.

Studies continue today about whether to build such a route, commonly known as Interstate 605, with latest concepts placing it somewhere east of the Sam-

JON WARREN / THE SEATTLE TIMES, 1988

rying 5,300 vehicles a day; the present count at the intersection with Highway 520 is nearly 40 times that number— more than 200,000 vehicles daily.

Within a few years after it was opened, the carefully designed 405/520 interchange had become one of the trickiest and most congested in the region, and by the 1990s it had to be rebuilt. A new flyover ramp leading traffic from 520 onto northbound 405 opened in 1993.

And while it was an engineering accomplishment when it opened in 1965, a section of elevated I-405 through Renton, known as the "S curves" because of its shape, required rebuilding in the 1980s and 1990s. The new section was finished in 1995 after 22 homes were removed.

I-405 also was affected by an abbreviation no one had thought of in the 1960s: HOV. Plans for high-occupancy-vehicle lanes began appearing in 1983, when the state Department of Transportation announced it would take five to seven years to build 15 miles of HOV lanes from Southcenter to Interstate 5.

In 2002, the final sections from Bothell to Lynnwood were finished. I-405 now has some 33 miles of HOV lanes, making it possible to drive from its south junction with I-5 at Tukwila to its north junction at Lynnwood without having to leave the car-pool lanes.

Inadequate from the start

Plans to expand the roadway capacity have been nearly constant since I-405 was started.

An I-405 Corridor Program study involving dozens of government agencies recommended a combination of mass-transit improvements and adding two general lanes for cars along the entire length of the highway route from Tukwila to Lynnwood.

As far as is known, no one has added up the costs of all the projects involved in building the freeway since 1948. Rebuilding the 405/520 interchange alone was estimated at $28 million, and redoing the S curves at $55 million.

The latest estimates for the cost of adding as many as two lanes in each direction are $9.1 billion to $10.9 billion.

Evening traffic lights up Bellevue's Northeast Eighth Street as comuters enter and exit from Interstate 405.

mamish Plateau.

A new Lake Washington bridge in the north part of the lake also was expected to be completed by 1990.

Neither the bridge nor the new highway was built.

Engineering marvel

Year by year, I-405 changed, and the conditions it operated in changed along with it. In 1960, it was car-

---

Sources include Washington State Department of Tranportation, Washington State Archives, and The East Side Journal.

CHAPTER 39

A BATTLE FOR OVERLAKE

The 13-year development war set the stage for a shift to a high-tech economy

This aerial photo shows the proposed Evergreen East area, now the main campus of Microsoft, with Overlake Shopping Center at the top.

GEOFF MANASSE / THE SEATTLE TIMES, 1980

S ome pieces of real estate are so much more important than their size would suggest. Evergreen East, for instance. A half-century ago it was a patch of second-growth forest halfway between Bellevue and Redmond. A few years later it touched off one of the most bitter land-use battles ever waged on the Eastside.

The outcome of that struggle shaped the region's economic future, solidifying Bellevue's position as its retail center and leading to Redmond's meteoric rise as the high-tech capital of the Northwest. Today the property is the main campus of Microsoft.

Real-estate vision

Few people foresaw the coming conflict or its ultimate significance when real-estate partners Bert McNae and Vic Rabel began acquiring pasture land and forest in a then-remote reach of East King County.

It was 1955, and McNae and Rabel were among many speculators and developers vying to reshape an area that had thrown off its old mining, logging and farming past but had not yet found a new identity.

In the post-World War II economic boom, Bellevue and other close-in communities were becoming bedroom suburbs of Seattle. Kemper Freeman Sr. opened

BY KEITH ERVIN

Bellevue Square, shown here in the late 1940s, expanded to a two-level mall after the demise of Evergreen East.

the Eastside's first shopping center, Bellevue Square, in 1946.

A few companies, such as Puget Sound Power & Light (now Puget Sound Energy), relocated their headquarters from Seattle to Bellevue to be closer to the homes of company executives and customers. But for the most part, the Eastside's new residents drove west across the Mercer Island floating bridge to jobs in Seattle.

McNae and Rabel anticipated that department stores soon would be scouting the farm-and-forest landscape for the best location to draw customers from the fast-growing Eastside. That location was Overlake, the geographic center of the area.

The investors announced in 1955 that they intended to develop a regional shopping center, a hospital, offices and manufacturing space on 520 acres.

Bert McNae

They called it Overlake Park, a name that has stuck in the shortened form of Overlake. The area now straddles the boundary of Bellevue and Redmond.

The investors' first step was to assemble land for a shopping center along 148th Avenue Northeast. The Bon Marché's parent company, Allied Stores, bought a portion of the land, and Sears and J.C. Penney also expressed interest in building stores.

Those plans were set back when state highway officials drew the route for Highway 520 smack through the shopping-center property.

Allied Stores kept the project alive by buying another property, along 156th Avenue Northeast south of Northeast 40th Street.

A 13-year battle erupted in 1968 when Allied announced its plans for a 120-acre shopping center — three times the area of Bellevue Square. They called the shopping center Evergreen East.

The Evergreen East war

The battle pitted the developers and the city of Redmond against Bellevue City Council opponents, neighborhood activists and Bellevue Square owners.

Redmond was eager to annex Evergreen East and rake in sales taxes from the shopping center. Some Bellevue City Council members favored the develop-

ment if boundaries could be drawn so Bellevue would get a significant share of the taxes.

But others warned that the shopping center would jeopardize not only Bellevue Square, but Bellevue itself.

"I believe that you can't locate two big behemoths next to each other and have both survive," says former Bellevue City Councilwoman Nancy Rising, recalling her arguments from the 1970s.

Downtown Bellevue was — and still is — highly unusual in that it is anchored by a modern shopping center. If Bellevue Square lost its biggest stores, Rising warned, "it's going to devastate everything."

Bellevue filed a legal challenge to Redmond's annexation of the site. During the controversy, Allied sold the project to Ohio mall developer Edward DeBartolo.

The rhetoric of the time still amazes McNae, who has retired to a condominium in Madison Park: "They talked about the pollution from too many automobiles. Imagine Bellevue talking about too many automobiles!"

Kemper Freeman Sr.

The fight ended in 1980, when the King County government declined to grant a grading permit on grounds that the project would generate too much traffic and air pollution.

Evergreen East's demise meant Bellevue Square operator Kemper Freeman Sr. and his son Kemper Freeman Jr. were able to launch a $100 million renovation that transformed their tired shopping center into one of the most successful, upscale malls in the nation.

The Bon, which tried for years to build at Overlake, opened a Bellevue Square store in 1984. Office developers built new skyscrapers within blocks.

A different direction

The death of Evergreen East freed up a large block of vacant land for high-tech development at Overlake — something McNae and his development partners had envisioned as early as 1955.

Redmond's first high-tech firm — Boeing spinoff United Control (now AlliedSignal) — moved from Seattle to Overlake in 1961. Rocket Research (now

Primex Aerospace), another Boeing spinoff, developed its own campus along Redmond's Willows Road in 1968, and the pace of high-tech development accelerated.

But the mother of all Eastside high-tech developments was to be the Evergreen East property. A corporate park opened on the site in 1983, drawing tenants with names like Microrim, Tektronix and McDonnell Douglas.

Then it landed a company that had outgrown its space in Bellevue: Microsoft. In 1986 Bill Gates' company built a cluster of buildings that resembled the X-wing fighters of "Star Wars" fame.

Since then, Microsoft has continually expanded, taking over all of the other buildings at Evergreen East and enlarging its campus to 260 acres. Microsoft has

EASTSIDE JOB GROWTH

	Population	Jobs
1970	197,043	38,945
1990	363,336	193,057
2000 (est.)	422,858	237,932

Source: Puget Sound Regional Council

also spilled across Highway 520 and now occupies about 40 Overlake buildings, with more on the way.

Microsoft is the chief economic engine of a high-tech industry that grew by nearly 15 percent annually from 1990 to 1995, compared with an overall employment increase of 2 percent here.

Today some 900 high-tech businesses employ more than 35,000 people on the Eastside.

No one can say for sure where Microsoft might have gone if the Evergreen East Shopping Center had not collapsed.

What is clear is that the property has become the storm center of an economic boom that has put Redmond on the international map and given the Eastside a clear identity at the beginning of a new century.

THE EASTSIDE'S ECONOMIC DEVELOPMENT

1860s

Coal mining begins in Newcastle and other towns. By the 1880s, Newcastle's population is second in King County, after Seattle.

1870s

A sawmill begins cutting plentiful timber in town of Donnelly on Lake Sammamish.

1910s

Vegetable and berry farms spread out from Bellevue to the Sammamish Valley.

1919

A sawmill on Mercer Slough shuts down after the last old-growth timber west of Lake Sammamish is logged.

1920s-30s

American Pacific Whaling's fleet operates out of Meydenbauer Bay and is for a time the area's biggest employer.

1940s

Navy contracts during World War II boost employment at Kirkland's Lake Washington Shipyards to 8,000. Farming declines as Japanese Americans are interned.

1946

Bellevue Square, the Eastside's first shopping center, opens to serve customers who previously shopped in Seattle.

1950s

Fast-growing populations turn Bellevue and Kirkland into bedroom suburbs of Seattle.

1961

Redmond's first major high-tech firm, United Control (now AlliedSignal), opens.

1986

Microsoft opens its first buildings at its current campus.

CHAPTER 40

EXCLUSIVELY EASTSIDE

Unique tidbits and legends make up a community's history

The first drive-in restaurant on the West Coast was in Renton. Mercer Island was the scene of the Eastside's first recorded murder. A rock festival blasted the ears of Woodinville residents, and both parties walked away unharmed from a duel in North Bend.

Fascinating historical tidbits and tales linger long after the chapters in this book were completed. What follows are a few of the more interesting ones.

Claim-jumping murder: Mercer Island pioneer James Colman argued with Enatai settler George Miller over illegal land claims. When Colman confronted him, Miller threatened to kill him if he came back.

On Feb. 8, 1886, Colman waved goodbye to his wife, Clarissa Colman, and left home with a 12-year-old house guest to row to Rainier Beach and catch a train from Seattle to Olympia, where he intended to file charges against Miller for claim-jumping.

A detective hired by Mrs. Colman later found their bodies and bloodstained rowboat near the south end of the island. The two had been shot.

After three trials, Miller ended up in jail for two years. He was acquitted and released. In the 1950s, Eastside historian Lucile McDonald interviewed Colman's daughter, Clarissa Colman Fawcett, who claimed Miller confessed to the murders on his deathbed. For many years, South Point on Mercer Island was called Murder Point by local residents.

High tide: Although Native Americans hunted on the island by day, when Thomas Mercer first began exploration there in the 1860s, local Indians refused to spend the night there. They had a legend that the island sank every night and rose again each morning.

Historians have speculated that legend may have roots in the sunken forests off Mercer Island shores.

The trees, standing upright, are at South Point and at the island's north end. They were a hazard to navigation, and around 1900 a ship and crew used a drag line to sheer off the tops to about 15-20 feet below the surface.

There are other submerged forests off St. Edward's Park in Kirkland and one in the south end of Lake Sammamish. Scientists believe a massive earthquake around 900 A.D. caused landslides that resulted in the underwater stands of trees.

Matzen Woolen Mills, on Kirkland's waterfront, burned down in 1935.

EASTSIDE HERITAGE CENTER

Chuck Berry played in a 1969 rock festival in Woodinville.

BY SHERRY GRINDELAND

Mine owners called in the Washington State Militia during labor unrest in 1891. The soldiers camped in Gilman, today's Issaquah.

Island castle: A tower was built for water storage on Mercer Island in 1889. It looked like a castle tower. Although it had long been abandoned, the landmark was destroyed in the early 1970s, when it was vandalized and then burned down.

Eastside rocks: Ike and Tina Turner, Chuck Berry, Guess Who and Led Zeppelin were some of the 25 performers who rocked at Woodinville's Gold Creek Park for three days beginning July 25, 1969.

More than 50,000 fans showed up for the Seattle Pop Festival, paying $6 a day or $15 for all three days. Crowds were so large that promoters had to bring in extra food and water.

Yes, some neighbors complained.

It's the law: The No. 1 ordinance in the city of Bothell, passed into law on Aug. 7, 1889, declared it unlawful for an ape or anyone dressed as an ape to appear on the streets of Bothell in July or August.

Apes ordinarily didn't wander the streets of Bothell. However, several people apparently dressed up as apes for the annual Mardi Gras festival.

The fine for such appearances was $5.

Army vs. miners: Labor problems occasionally surfaced at Eastside mines. Owners called in the Washington State Militia to prevent violence in 1891. At least one troop camped in Gilman, today's Issaquah, for two weeks while things cooled off.

Material matters: One of the first wool mills in Washington, Matzen Woolen Mills, was on the waterfront near today's Marina Park in Kirkland. It burned

The castle tower, a Mercer Island landmark, was built in 1889.

down in a spectacular fire in 1935.

Floating club: The first American Legion Hall in Kirkland was a World War I surplused Liberty Ship, permanently moored at the waterfront. The cannons that once marked the Kirkland city limits on Lake Washington Boulevard were also WWI surplus. They stood at the corner of Lake Washington Boulevard and

The vessel Port Jackson was used as a clubhouse for the Warren O. Grimm Post of the American Legion in Kirkland.

10th Avenue South. Eventually they were moved to the Redmond American Legion Hall.

Walking the plank: In the early 1900s, a puncheon or wooden walkway ran along the Lake Washington waterfront from Houghton to Kirkland.

Dueling friends: In Ada S. Hill's "History of the Snoqualmie Valley," pioneer Annie Carpenter told of two drunken men, Mike McGilvey and a Mr. McGowan, who got into a fierce argument in the late 1800s. They were so angry, they decided to have a duel.

Accompanied by friends, they went to a field near Tollgate Farm and were each given a rifle. They counted out the paces, turned around and pulled the triggers.

Silence.

The friends had not loaded the guns. The surprised duelers were so happy they laughed and hugged one another.

Popular site: When the first railroad excursion brought sightseers to Snoqualmie Falls in June 1889, entertainment included a tightrope walker traversing the falls on a high wire. The local citizens had prepared food for 400-500 people, but more than 1,000 came and the food ran out. The following weekend, the citizens prepared for a large influx. But sales were down — word had gotten around in Seattle, and the tourists brought their own food.

Bear baby: In the 1870s, Redmond pioneers Warren and Laura Perrigo built the Melrose House, an inn for travelers not far from today's Bear Creek Shopping Center. For about three weeks, visitors were entertained by the antics of a bear cub.

The Perrigos' hired hand, DeWhitt Griswold, captured the bear while he was hunting. According to Redmond historian Nancy Way, Griswold tied it to the woodshed and gave it a barrel for a bed.

Each morning the bear would pull out the straw from the barrel and air it, then put the straw back into the barrel at night. The bear eventually chewed through the rope leash and escaped.

Playing train: Willowmoor Farm, what is today's Marymoor Park, had its own narrow-gauge steam railroad to move grain, feed, other supplies and workers between the more than two dozen sheds, barns and outbuildings.

Long service: Bill Brown was practically mayor for life. He was elected mayor of Redmond in 1918 and

Redmond's Marymoor Park is on the site of J.W. Clise's Willowmoor Farm.

served until 1948.

He was also a King County commissioner from 1924-32, and one of his projects was getting West Lake Sammamish Parkway built. (Brown also benefited from the highway project. It opened up access to two of his developments: Rosemont and Rosemont Beach.)

Bill Brown

Waterless watershed: Although it is still known as the Redmond Watershed, it hasn't produced a drop of drinking water for at least 70 years.

Redmond purchased the land and Seidel Creek in 1926 to provide water to a thirsty town. Several years later, the state health department determined the water didn't meet state safety standards and the waterworks was shut down. Today the open space contains popular biking and hiking trails.

Farm industry: Union Hill in Redmond was home to at least 15 mink ranches in the 1950s. In the Sammamish Valley, there were 25 dairy farms in 1948. But Redmond's biggest farming export was baby chicks. Poultry farms and hatcheries were numerous. Even after farmers gave up raising chickens locally, Redmond's H & N International hatched and shipped 8 million chicks a year in the 1980s.

Mascot meaning: When Native American Henry Moses played basketball for Renton High School in 1916, competitors from other schools jeered, calling the Renton team a bunch of Indians.

Moses, whose family lived in the area before Caucasian settlers arrived, said the name-calling was a positive thing because Indians stand for determination,

RENTON HISTORICAL SOCIETY

Native American Henry Moses played basketball at Renton High School in 1916.

bravery and strength.

When the basketball team won the state championship that year, the school voted to be permanently known as the Indians. Moses, a talented athlete, went on to briefly play professional baseball.

Mugged: Root beer became a hot commodity when the Triple XXX Barrel drive-in restaurant opened in Renton in the mid-1930s. It was the first drive-in on the West Coast.

CHAPTER 41

EASTSIDE TODAY

From pioneer roots to high-tech powerhouse, it's a good place to call home

ELLEN BANNER / THE SEATTLE TIMES, 2001

Luke McRedmond wouldn't recognize the place.

When he left Seattle in the spring of 1871 for a new life east of Lake Washington, McRedmond and his family had to contend with angry Indians and a back-wrenching pioneer life on the Sammamish River plain.

One hundred thirty-one years later, the McRedmond homestead is an upscale mall, and the city that bears the family name is proud home of a software company whose annual sales surpass the revenue of small countries.

Welcome to the Eastside, 2002.

With the Cascade Mountains in the background, this view from the hillside above Interstate 90 shows the Bellevue skyline.

Since arrival of the first pioneers, the Eastside has metamorphosed numerous times. Logging ground. Homestead. Farm. City-dweller's getaway. Bedroom community. And finally, a self-standing population center with a hard-revving economic engine of its own.

Today it is also a place that is wrestling over its future, trying to balance the desire to be a financial powerhouse as well as a good place to call home, one that retains the natural assets that made it so appealing in the first place.

The Eastside has long played a supporting role to Seattle, but in the 21st century that position as second-fiddle no longer seems apt. The Eastside today is 18 incorporated cities from Bothell to Renton to Snoqualmie, with 539,000 people — roughly equal to the population of Seattle.

It has become a place of remarkable economic strength.

BY CHRIS SOLOMON

Lake Sammamish State Park in Issaquah provides many recreational opportunities.

Nearly half of the Eastside's "covered employment" — the workforce excluding the military, farmhands and the self-employed — is in the high-tech industry, finance, insurance, real estate or related services, according to a report by the Puget Sound Regional Council. (One caveat: PSRC's report does not count the Eastside's easternmost, rural communities as part of the Eastside.) High-tech jobs were as likely to be on the Eastside as in Seattle, according to King County's annual growth report.

A bedroom metropolis? No more. In 1980, about one in seven jobs in King County was on the Eastside, and more people slept here than worked here. Today the Eastside is home to 28 percent of county jobs, and more people come here to work than live here.

Warehouse giant Costco, truck-maker Paccar, apparel maker Eddie Bauer and dozens of lesser-known but highly successful private companies all have their headquarters on the Eastside. Microsoft, the Eastside's single largest employer, has about 23,000 jobs on and around its Redmond campus.

Affluence has followed the white-collar jobs and computer industry. In 2000, the Eastside's average household income was $105,000, versus $72,000 in Seattle.

Yet despite the area's seeming clout, observers frequently remark that the Eastside still is a place that has yet to fully learn how to flex its political muscle.

The peace that once lured picnickers from Seattle across Lake Washington is still there for those residents who seek it. City parks are plentiful and handsome, and the mossy forests of the Issaquah Alps and Mount Baker-Snoqualmie National Forest are a quick drive away. Another sense of serenity also lures people: The Eastside has good public schools,

Paragliding is popular at Tiger Mountain near Issaquah.

and violent crime is low. Residents of Bellevue, to take one city, frequently report they are happy with city services.

Diversity has come more slowly than in big cities like Seattle, but it is increasing apace. Bellevue is now more than 17 percent Asian, according to 2000 U.S. Census statistics.

More than 60 languages are spoken in the Bellevue School District. As newcomers arrive, the tapestry of the Eastside grows less monochrome. Still, many of the cities remain overwhelmingly white.

Despite the progress and rosy outlook, the Eastside has its share of challenges, and some of them are quite daunting.

For example, the world's richest man lives a few miles from food banks that give out canned corn to immigrant families who cannot make ends meet.

People love their automobiles yet complain bitterly about how bad traffic has become on Interstate 405 and the bridges across Lake

Highway 520 provides access to Microsoft's Redmond campus.

Washington.

Salaries are large, yet the lack of affordable housing consistently ranks right behind traffic as a top concern of residents and employers.

For some people, the Eastside is not a place in the heart. The area is sometimes unfavorably compared to the suburbs of Southern California: cities in search of a community spirit, a character.

Some pin their hopes on newer-style housing developments such as Issaquah Highlands and Snoqualmie Ridge now appearing on the Eastside. By rearranging houses to encourage interaction between families, by including amenities such as stores within walking distance of home, these massive subdivisions are supposed to reconnect residents with each other, and with their neighborhood. The jury is still out.

Others hope that vitality will flourish in places like downtown Kirkland and Bellevue, where new apartment buildings and promenades with shops are already starting to spur downtown life.

But not everyone is thrilled about such changes. As the amount of buildable land on the Eastside shrinks (thanks to growth-management laws that are trying to keep houses off farmland and out of forest), the pressure grows on some neighborhoods to become more dense and urban.

On the Eastside, nothing brings out residents faster than when the City Council considers tinkering with the zoning to allow an apartment building.

Trying to protect the natural beauty that first attracted residents is an ongoing struggle. Around Sammamish and Snoqualmie, farms and forestlands stand beside new subdivisions.

Landmark deals such as a $185 million agreement to protect the 104,000-acre Weyerhaeuser's Snoqualmie Tree Farm from development will keep in place hunks of the green landscape that people came here for. Still, preservationists see the area dying a death of a thousand cuts, with every new home that appears in rural areas.

Clearly, Eastsiders will continue to wrestle over how to get more elbow room, without elbowing out nature.

And what would old Luke McRedmond think about the changes? One supposes he'd be proud, surely, at his prescience when he spied a future in the Sammamish's rich river dirt.

ANDREA J. WRIGHT / THE SEATTLE TIMES, 2000

Children are attracted to the outdoor artwork at Kirkland's Marina Park.

JIMI LOTT / THE SEATTLE TIMES, 2000

The Bellevue Art Museum, which opened in 2001, offers 5,800 square feet of gallery space.

Primarily a residential center now, Newcastle incorporated in 1994 but had its origins in coal mining.

JIM BATES / THE SEATTLE TIMES, 2002

CHAPTER 42

TIME TRAVELING

Take an afternoon to tour the history that lingers around the Eastside

Remnants of the Eastside's rich and many-layered history are scattered throughout the area — reminders of once-flourishing towns long since disappeared, formerly dynamic industries and pioneer life that planted the seeds for what was to come. Using the list below, take an afternoon, a map and your imagination as you explore these pages of Eastside history.

Numbered items correspond to map on page 131

THE SEATTLE TIMES, 1969

The Beckstrom Log Cabin

1 BOTHELL LANDING, 9919 N.E. 180th St. Once the stopping place for steamboats on the Sammamish River, the landing now showcases three historic homes and the original Bothell schoolhouse. The Bothell Historical Museum (open from 1-4 p.m. Sundays) is in the former home of pioneer William A. Hannan. The Beckstrom Log Cabin was built in 1883 by Swedish immigrant Andrew Beckstrom and his wife, Augusta, and they lived in it while homesteading on 160 acres just north of Bothell. Also on the site is Lytle House, the home of Dr. Elmer Ellsworth Lytle, who moved to Bothell in 1898. The Bothell schoolhouse was built in 1885 and was restored after being used as a private residence. Phone: 425-486-1889.

2 BOTHELL PIONEER CEMETERY, Valley View Road and Northeast 180th Street, was laid out in 1889. Many of the city's founders, including David and Mary Ann Bothell, are buried there. The Bothells' tombstone is at right.

3 WOODINVILLE PIONEER CEMETERY, Woodinville-Snohomish Road and Northeast 175th Street. Ira Woodin officially donated one acre for the community cemetery in 1898, although it had been the town's informal burial ground

SEATTLE TIMES, 1990

as early as 1888. Several early pioneers are buried there, including Ira and Susan Woodin. Phone: 425-483-3759.

4 HOLLYWOOD SCHOOLHOUSE •, 14810 N.E. 145th St., Woodinville. Built in 1912, it replaced a smaller building destroyed by fire. Materials for the schoolhouse were donated by lumber tycoon Frederick Stimson, the owner of Hollywood Farm. Hours: 9 a.m. to 5 p.m. Monday through Friday; also available as a party hall. Phone: 425-481-7925. *www.hollywoodschoolhouse.com.*

5 HOLLYWOOD FARM * +, 14111 N.E. 145th St., Woodinville. The former 206-acre dairy farm and country estate of Seattle lumberman Frederick Stimson was built from 1910-13. His wife, Nellie, grew flowers that were sold in Honolulu and Nome, Alaska. The original mansion and carriage house are today part of the Chateau Ste. Michelle Winery.

6 SHUMWAY MANSION, 11410 99th Place N.E., Kirkland. This 1909 mansion was moved from downtown Kirkland to Juanita in 1985 by an investment group led by Richard and Salli Harris and turned into a bed-and-breakfast and reception center. The 18-room New England-style house was home of Carrie Shumway and her family.

In 1911, Shumway was elected the first city councilwoman in the state. She and her sisters founded several Seattle clubs; she taught school in Tokyo and

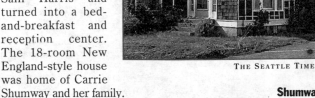

THE SEATTLE TIMES, 1983

Shumway Mansion before its move to Juanita

Key: * King County Landmark. • On the State Register of Historic Places. + On the National Register of Historic Places.

COMPILED BY SHERRY GRINDELAND

Eastside historical sites

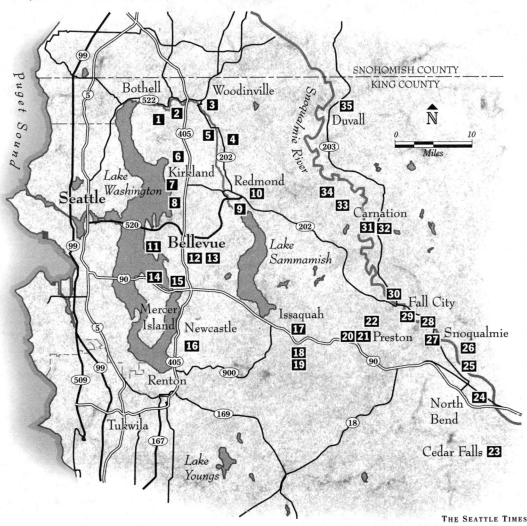

THE SEATTLE TIMES

she helped found the Kirkland Women's Club. Hours: 10 a.m. to 6 p.m. Monday through Friday. Phone: 425-823-2303.

THE SEATTLE TIMES, 1985

7 PETER KIRK BUILDING +, 620 Market St., Kirkland. City founder Peter Kirk hoped to turn the Moss Bay area into a steel-production center. He built an ironworks and steel mill, and set up the Kirkland Land and Improvement Co. to sell lots to settlers and workers. His office was on the second floor of the Peter Kirk Building, above a mercantile and drugstore. The mill never produced any metal, but from his second-floor office in the 1889 building, Kirk launched the town that would be named after him. The Peter Kirk Building is now home of the Kirkland Arts Center. Hours: 11 a.m. to 6 p.m. Monday through Friday. Phone: 425-823-7176.

Several nearby homes were built by Kirk's company around 1889. On 10th Avenue West look for three old two-story homes, now private residences, including a couple of red-brick houses similar to the Peter Kirk Building. Two homes on Eighth Avenue West are also from the same era.

8 CARILLON POINT, on Lake Washington Boulevard near the entrance to Yarrow Bay in Kirkland. A hotel, office complex and a marina opened on this site in 1989, but more than 100 years earlier, in 1883, James Curtis, his wife and their two sons built a large house south of today's hotel that was also a traveler's waystop. The Curtis men, along with others, began building boats for travel on Lake Washington and Lake Sammamish.

Key: * King County Landmark. • On the State Register of Historic Places. + On the National Register of Historic Places.

The Clise Mansion, built in 1904, now houses the Eastside Heritage Center/ Marymoor Museum.

THE SEATTLE TIMES, 1986

In 1901 Capt. George Bartsch and Harry Tompkins opened a small shipyard at the site of today's complex. By 1908 it had become Anderson Shipbuilding. During World Wars I and II, the shipyards were part of the war effort. Between the two wars, the facility was used to repair fishing vessels. The shipyards closed in 1946.

9 **MARYMOOR PARK**, 6046 W. Lake Sammamish Parkway N.E., Redmond. The site of this 762-acre park was homesteaded in 1875 by John and Adam Tosh, and became James Clise's Willowmoor Farm in 1904. It was a model dairy farm and summer retreat. The 28-room Tudor-style Clise Mansion, built as a hunting lodge for Anna and James Clise in 1904, today houses the Eastside Heritage Center/Marymoor Museum. Museum hours are 11 a.m. to 4 p.m. Tuesdays, Wednesdays and Thursdays, 1-4 p.m. Sundays, and by appointment. Phone: 425-885-3684. *www.eastsideheritagecenter.org.*

The site was also popular with Native Americans, who camped along the shores of Lake Sammamish and the Sammamish River. Archaeological research is described on a large sign between the slough and the mansion.

10 **RED BRICK ROAD • * +**, 196th Avenue Northeast between Union Hill Road and Redmond-Fall City Road, Redmond. Also known as the James Mattson Road and Old Brick Road, this 18-foot-wide, 2.3-mile brick stretch is the only unaltered section of historic Yellowstone Trail left in King County. It was built in 1910 and resurfaced with brick in 1913, and was one of four cross-country routes between the Atlantic and Pacific oceans. The Red Brick Road went farther than Yellowstone, actually connecting Seattle to Boston.

THE SEATTLE TIMES, 1977

Medina City Hall and Municipal Court

11 **MEDINA FERRY DOCK •**, 501 Evergreen Point Road, Medina. Built in 1913, the Medina City Hall building of today once accommodated passengers waiting for a ferry ride that would take them across the lake to Leschi in Seattle. The building is open to the public from 8:30 a.m. to 5 p.m. Phone: 425-454-9222.

12 **WILBURTON TRESTLE +,** just east of Interstate 405 in Bellevue, spans Mercer Slough next to Southeast Eighth Street. Built by the Northern Pacific Railroad in 1904 at nearly 100 feet above the ground and 984 feet long, it is the lone local remnant of numerous trestles and bridges built during the heyday of railroading.

13 **KELSEY CREEK PARK**, 13204 S.E. Eighth Place, Bellevue. The Frazer Cabin, the first permanent home in Bellevue, is on display in the park. Daniel William Frazer hired two Norwegian woodsmen to build the house as a wedding present for his sister and her husband. Two large white barns and a farmhouse, now home to the Bellevue Parks Department, remain from the original 79-acre dairy farm. Farm hours: 9:30 a.m. to 3:30 p.m. daily. Phone: 425-452-7688.

14 **LUTHER BURBANK SCHOOL ***, 2040 84th Ave. S.E., Mercer Island. Started in 1903 as a school for truants, it had become a boys reformatory by 1914 and included a hospital, laundry and large barn. Boys went to school half a day and the rest of the time worked in the gardens and orchards and cared for the livestock. Of the many buildings, only a brick dormitory remains. The facility had several names including the Boys Parental School, until it became Luther Burbank School in 1931. In 1966, students were moved to Echo Glen Children's Center in Preston. The site later became a park.

15 **WINTERS HOUSE +,** 2102 Bellevue Way S.E., Bellevue. The home that now houses the Bellevue Historical Society was built for Frederick and Cecilia Winters in the late 1920s in the then-popular Spanish style with a tile roof and stucco. The couple operated a rhododendron nursery and sold azaleas, daffodils and irises. The city of Bellevue purchased the 13-room house for $1.7 million in 1990 and spent $365,000 restoring it. Phone: 425-452-5606.

16 **NEWCASTLE CEMETERY •,** (circa 1870), 129th Avenue Southeast near Lake Boren. Newcastle, once the second-largest town in Washington, attracted coal miners from around the world during its boom period of 1884 to 1898. In death the miners and their families were divided into ethnic groups in the 2.2-acre cemetery, which has been preserved by the Newcastle Historical Society. The cemetery is on the west side of 129th just north of Lake Boren Park.

Key: * King County Landmark. **•** On the State Register of Historic Places. **+** On the National Register of Historic Places.

Open from dawn to dusk between Memorial Day and Labor Day, or by appointment. Phone: 425-226-4238.

THE SEATTLE TIMES, 1980

Pickering Farm Barn

17 PICKERING FARM BARN, 1730 10th Ave. N.W. Issaquah, near Costco. All that remains of the Pickering Farm, once the largest dairy farm in the Issaquah area, is the 1878 barn. A concrete floor and foundation were added in 1994. Note the notched vertical beams and side beams, from old-growth fir, that are attached with beveled wooden pegs. Hours: 9 a.m. to 2 p.m. during the Farmers' Market between April and October; available for rental. Phone: 425-837-3321.

18 ISSAQUAH DEPOT, 50 Rainier Blvd. N., Issaquah. Built for the town of Gilman in 1889, the depot became a gathering spot each afternoon when the mail arrived. (The town was renamed Issaquah and incorporated in 1892.) Trains carried coal, lumber and dairy products from the surrounding valleys. The depot was the first building in town to receive electricity and operated until the 1950s. In 1984, the Issaquah Historical Society acquired the depot and has since restored it. Volunteers have also been restoring old rail cars. The depot is open from 11 a.m. to 3 p.m. Fridays through Sundays. Phone: 425-392-3500. *www.issaquahhistory.org.*

The Gilman Town Hall was built in the 1880s.

19 GILMAN TOWN HALL, 165 N.E. Andrews St., Issaquah. The Issaquah Historical Society uses Gilman's original town hall as a museum. Check out the photo collection, memorabilia from the turn of the century and the old blockhouse jail behind the town hall. The building is open from 11 a.m. to 3 p.m. Thursdays through Saturdays. Phone: 425-392-3500. *www.issaquahhistory.org.*

THE SEATTLE TIMES, 1997

20 LOVEGREN HOUSE *, 8612 310th Ave. S.E., Preston. This 1904 home was built in the neoclassic style for local lumber baron August Lovegren. (This is a private residence.)

21 PRESTON MILL SITE, corner of Preston-Fall City Road Southeast and Upper Preston Road, has been acquired by King County for a park. The mill was built in 1892 by August Lovegren to meet demand for cedar shingles after the Great Seattle Fire of 1889. Atop two stumps at the entrance is a large section of log marked with the words "Preston Mill."

22 RAGING RIVER BRIDGE *, Southeast 68th Street off Preston-Fall City Road Southeast, was built in 1915. The 70-foot-long structure, designed by Daniel Benjamin Luten, is on an abandoned spur of Preston-Fall City Road Southeast. It was reinforced in 1995.

23 CEDAR FALLS, Cedar Falls Road Southeast (follow to the end of the road and hike along a trail to town), southeast of Rattlesnake Lake, North Bend. The town of Cedar Falls was built by Seattle City Light to house construction workers for its first power plant at Chester Morse Dam. Once a large company town, deer and elk now graze near the dilapidated tennis courts. Several houses and original streetlights remain. Open weekdays only.

24 TOLLGATE FARM, Highway 202, just west of North Bend, was founded in the late 1800s by Jeremiah Borst, the first permanent white settler in the Upper Snoqualmie Valley. The farm was named after the nearby toll bridge that crossed the South Fork of the Snoqualmie River. A small stockade, known as Fort Smalley, predated the farm. Fort Smalley's blockhouses and enclosure were built during the Indian uprising of 1855-56.

Several parts of the Tollgate Farm have been purchased and set aside for parks and open space since 2000, thanks to a partnership between the city of North Bend, King County and the Trust for Public Land.

25 MEADOWBROOK FARM, near North Bend Boulevard North and Northwest 14th Street, has been acquired by King County for park land. It was a hop farm in the 1880s, and a popular berry-picking and trading place for Native American groups before the arrival of white settlers. The site contains several unmarked graves of former chiefs.

26 REINIG ROAD SYCAMORE CORRIDOR *, and the lost town of Snoqualmie Falls, between 396th Drive Southeast and Southeast 79th Street, northeast of Snoqualmie. Snoqualmie Falls was built nearby in 1916-17 to house loggers and mill workers. The sycamore trees were planted as part of a 1929 beautification program. Weyerhaeuser later dismantled the town.

27 SNOQUALMIE DEPOT + *, 38625 S.E. King St., Snoqualmie. Built in 1889-90 by the Seattle,

Key: * King County Landmark. • On the State Register of Historic Places. + On the National Register of Historic Places.

The Snoqualmie Depot

Lake Shore & Eastern Railway, this city landmark was donated by Burlington Northern to the Puget Sound Railroad Historical Association. An interpretive sign next to the log pavilion on King Street, a half-block west of the depot, tells the 1890s boomtown history. Hours: 10:15 a.m. to 5 p.m.. Thursdays through Mondays. Phone: 425-888-3030. *www.trainmuseum.org.*

28 FORT TILTON, Turn right onto Fish Hatchery Road from Highway 202 just east of Fall City and follow it to the Snoqualmie River. A sign on the narrow bank above the river notes the site of the 1850s fort. It was one of three forts built in the Snoqualmie Valley for protection against Indians and the only one actually ever used as a fort, with soldiers stationed there in March 1856.

29 FALL CITY CEMETERY, on Southeast 47th Street south of Fall City. The first burial was in the mid-1870s. It is the resting place of many Snoqualmie Valley pioneers, including Josiah "Si" Merritt, after whom Mount Si is named, and Jeremiah Borst, considered the father of the Snoqualmie Valley. Also buried here are numerous members of the Snoqualmie Tribe, including "Grandma," whose grave marker notes she was 130 years old, and tribal elder Ed Davis, who died in 1987 at age 110.

Fall City Hop Shed

30 FALL CITY HOP SHED * •, at a riverfront park about a quarter-mile north of Fall City on Highway 203. Cash from hops kept Eastside farming communities green in the late 1880s. Hops were dried in sheds and then shipped to England. The Fall City Hop Shed is the only one left. It was built in 1889 by George Davis Rutherford and measures 20 feet by 20 feet. The shed was moved to its current location in 1904 from near the Sno-

qualmie River. Phone: 425-222-7484.

31 TOLT ODDFELLOWS/EAGLES HALL *, 3940 Tolt Ave., Carnation. An 1895 two-story frame building, it was used as a social hall and Snoqualmie Indians tribal headquarters for several years.

32 HJERTOOS FARM *•+, 31523 N.E. 40th St., Carnation. This Victorian house was built in 1907 by dairy farmers Andrew and Bergette Hjertoos, who were Norwegian immigrants. A great-grandson, Roger Thorson, has restored the home and barn. Thorson now runs a Christmas tree farm on the property. *www.carnation-treefarm.com.*

33 VINCENT SCHOOL HOUSE AND COMMUNITY CLUB *, 8010 W. Snoqualmie Valley Road N.E., Carnation. In 1905 the townsfolk of Vincent taxed themselves to build this wood-framed, gable-roofed school building on donated land. It is now owned by the Vincent Community Club. Tours and rentals are available by appointment: 425-788-6083.

34 QUAALE LOG HOUSE, 10101 W. Snoqualmie Valley Road N.E., Carnation. Built in 1907, this private residence is the only intact historic log house in the valley.

35 DOUGHERTY FARM *, 26526 N.E. Cherry Valley Road, Duvall. Built in 1888 on the Snoqualmie River, the house was moved — along with much of the town of Cherry Valley — in 1909 when the Chicago, Milwaukee and St. Paul Railroad needed the land. In 1984 the Duvall Historical Society began a now-complete restoration of the T-shaped wood-frame house. Tours available by appointment. Phone: 425-788-1266.

The Hjertoos Farm in the early 1900s

Key: * King County Landmark. **•** On the State Register of Historic Places. **+** On the National Register of Historic Places.

HISTORICAL ORGANIZATIONS

Bellevue Historical Society
2102 Bellevue Way S.E.
(Winters House)
Bellevue, WA 98004
425-450-1046

Bothell Historical Museum Society
9919 N.E. 180th St.
Bothell, WA 98041
425-486-1889

Center for Puget Sound History and Archaeology
Bellevue Community College
3000 Landerholm Circle S.E.
Bellevue, WA 98007
www.bcc.ctc.edu/cpsha/default.htm

Duvall Historical Society
P.O. Box 385
Duvall, WA 98019
425-788-6209

Issaquah Historical Society
Gilman Town Hall Museum
165 S.E. Andrews St.
Issaquah, WA 98027
425-392-3500
P.O. Box 695
Issaquah, WA 98027
www.issaquahhistory.org

Kenmore Heritage Society
P.O. Box 82027
Kenmore, WA 98028
425-488-2818
www.scn.org/civic/kenmoreheritage/

King County Landmarks & Heritage Program
Smith Tower
506 Second Ave., Suite 200
Seattle, WA 98104
206-296-7580
www.metrokc.gov/exec/culture/heritage/index.htm

Kirkland Heritage Society
1032 Fourth St.
Kirkland, WA 98003
425-828-4095

Eastside Heritage Center/Marymoor Museum
6046 W. Lake Sammamish Parkway N.E.
Redmond, WA 98052
425-885-3684
www.eastsiderheritagecenter.org

Mercer Island Historical Society
9611 36th Ave. S.E.
Mercer Island, WA 98040
P.O. Box 111 (mailing address)
Mercer Island, WA 98040
206-232-6187
www.mihistory.org

Newcastle Historical Society
7105 138th Ave. S.E. (mailing)
Newcastle, WA 98059
Newcastle City Hall (meetings)
13020 S.E. 72nd Place, Suite A
Newcastle, WA 98059
425-226-4238

Northwest Railway Museum
P.O. Box 459
Snoqualmie, WA 98065
425-888-0373
www.trainmuseum.org

Pioneer Association of the State of Washington
1642 43rd Ave. E.
Seattle, WA 98112
206-325-0888
www.wapioneers.org

Puget Sound Maritime Historical Society
2700 24th Ave. E.
Seattle, WA 98112
206-324-1125
www.pugetmaritime.org

Renton Historical Society
Renton Museum
235 Mill Ave. S.
Renton, WA 98005
425-255-2330

Redmond Historical Society
Old Redmond Schoolhouse Community Center
16600 N.E. 80th St.
Room 106
Redmond, WA 98073
425-885-2919
www.redmondhistory.org

Sammamish Historical Society
704 228th Ave. N.E.
PMB# 2222
Sammamish, WA 98074
425-281-0170
425-392-2446

Snoqualmie Valley Historical Society
P.O. Box 179 (Mailing)
320 Bendigo Blvd. S.
North Bend, WA 98045
425-888-3200
www.snoqualmievalleymuseum.org

Tolt Historical Society
P.O. Box 91 (mailing)
Carnation, WA 98014
Sno-Valley Senior Center (meeting)
4610 Stevens Ave.
Carnation, WA 98014
425-333-4436

Woodinville Heritage Society
P.O. Box 216
Woodinville, WA 98072
425-483-8270